P9-DDF-675

By Michele Stuart
Perfect Pies
Perfect Pies & More

perfect pies
& more

perfect pies & more

All New Pies, Cookies, Bars, and Cakes

from America's Pie-Baking Champion

MICHELE STUART

Ballantine Books
New York

Published in the United States by Ballantine Books, an imprint of The Random House Publishing Group, a division of Random House, Inc., New York.

BALLANTINE and the HOUSE colophon are registered trademarks of Random House, Inc.

Library of Congress Cataloging-in-Publication Data
Stuart, Michele.
  Perfect pies & more : all new pies, cookies, bars, and cakes from America's pie-baking champion / Michele Stuart.
    pages cm
  Includes index.
  ISBN 978-0-345-54419-3 (hardcover : acid-free paper)—ISBN 978-0-345-54420-9 (ebook)
  1. Pies 2. Desserts. I. Title. II. Title: Perfect pies and more.
  TX773.S914 2013
  641.86'52—dc23   2013009622

Printed in China

www.ballantinebooks.com

9 8 7 6 5 4 3 2 1

First Edition

Book design by Diane Hobbing

For my dad, the man who
taught me everything I know
about strength and dedication

Contents

Introduction

It would be almost impossible to explain how grateful I am that I get to spend each day doing the things I love most: baking pies and being a business owner, a wife, and a mom. As if all of that weren't enough, I also get to write a second cookbook. Whereas my first book, *Perfect Pies,* focused entirely on pies, this time around I've expanded my scope to include not only pies, but also my favorite breads, bars, cookies, and a range of other sweet treats. In this cookbook, you'll find that the emphasis is on ease and efficiency.

Writing a cookbook requires large blocks of concentrated, uninterrupted time—hours upon hours to create the recipes, test the recipes, and write them down, and time to reflect on why these recipes in particular are important to me and worthy of being included in a cookbook. With that in mind, last summer I decided to sneak away from my two Michele's Pies bakeries in Connecticut for a couple of weeks so that I could concentrate on writing this book. I left both branches of Michele's Pies in the competent hands of my husband, Kelly, and took our son Dakota with me up to our ski condo in Vermont. While Dakota was at camp during the days, I worked in the condo's little kitchen on the recipes you'll find in this book. Before I set up shop in Connecticut, all I had was this tiny home kitchen in Vermont where I would bake my pies and other treats to sell at local farmer's markets.

As I dusted off my favorite Le Creuset saucepan and pie dish and stood at the kitchen counter rolling out dough or cutting out cookies, I found myself reflecting on how far I'd come and how much my process has changed over the years. Although I bake every single day in my pie shops, there's a big difference between cooking in a commercial kitchen and cooking at home. In many ways, those couple of weeks in Vermont offered me a wonderful opportunity to simplify and remember how I used to bake in the earliest days of Michele's Pies. On the other hand, it reminded me that there are certain considerations home bakers have to deal with that I don't have to take into account in the shop, such as inconsistent oven temperatures and a general lack of space.

I'm at a point in my life where things are busier than ever. While I wouldn't change anything, I often find that there just aren't enough hours in the day. Running a business, being a good mom and wife, and preparing for a new baby (did I mention I was also pregnant while writing this book?) doesn't leave a lot of time to spare. For as much as I love baking, I find that I have less and less time to dedicate to any one project. I take pies and other sweet treats very seriously, so I will never be okay with sacrificing quality; but sometimes when it comes to the actual baking process, simpler is better and a few shortcuts are okay.

In this uninterrupted time of baking and reflection in Vermont, with nostalgic aromas filling up the kitchen, I also had a lot of time to think about family. It's amazing how smelling a cookie your mom used to bake when you were a child or biting into a pie just like Grandma's can transport you back in time and bring a warm rush of memories. I also thought about how happy I am not only that I now get to share all of these traditions with my own growing family, but also that we are creating new memories of our own. I hope that someday Dakota will bite into a slice of Maple Pecan Cake (page 193) and it will remind him of those summer weeks the two of us spent together in Vermont in 2012.

In thinking about the home baker, I've taken great care to gear all of these recipes to home ovens that may be just as "quirky" as the one in my own Vermont kitchen. People always ask me about cooking times, and sometimes they tell me that it takes more or less time to bake a pie in their kitchen than a recipe specifies. Being back in Vermont reminded me that kitchen ovens can be a bit unpredictable; the temperatures aren't moderated and stable like the commercial variety I tend to use these days. With this in mind, my number-one suggestion for any home baker is to always use a separate oven thermometer placed on a rack in the oven. This way you'll always know at precisely what temperature you're really baking your desserts—and this number is often *not* the same as the temperature you've set your oven at. Also, you'll notice that a lot of these recipes give a range of baking times to allow for differently calibrated ovens. I've provided visual cues to look for so that you can gauge when a pie or treat is done.

Although there are recipes of all levels of difficulty in this book, I think you'll find that many of them are on the easier side and even allow for a few shortcuts that help guarantee lots of great homemade treats for your family, even if you don't have a ton of time. I've indicated the level of difficulty for each recipe so that you have a good idea of how much time and effort it will require before you get started. That way, if you're looking for a quick fix you can select an easy recipe. If you want to spend a bit more time in the kitchen, it's a great opportunity to try a challenging recipe. To give you a clear idea of what these different levels entail:

Easy: 1 hour or less prep time
Moderate: 1 to 2 hours prep time
Challenging: 2 hours or more prep time

Also, I always recommend that you read through a recipe in its entirety *before* beginning, so that you have a clear understanding of all the steps and how the recipe will come together.

On the following pages I've shared many of my favorite pies, tea breads, cookies, bars, and other sweet treats in the hopes that you can also incorporate them into your own family's traditions. Of course, there is a wide selection of pies, including everything from the simple Peach-Strawberry Crumb Pie (page 38) to the whimsical Thin Mint Chocolate Cookie Pie (page 116). This time I didn't just stop at pies, though. You'll also find a selection of other treats that I either carry in my stores or enjoy making for my own family. From Pumpkin Bread (page 195) to Blueberry-Blackberry Turnovers (page 209) to Snickerdoodle Cookies (page 162), there really is something for everyone in this book. And, since I was pregnant while writing this book, you'll find lots and lots of chocolate!

Putting these recipes together reminded me of their origins—many of them came from my childhood, and others have become a part of my own family's tradition today. Although I love indulging in pies and treats, what I love most is the bonding experience they provide with loved ones, and how they become a deliciously tactile way of keeping memories alive. I've shared some of my own fond memories within these pages, but my greatest hope is that you and your loved ones will create your own memories and traditions around these cherished recipes as well.

perfect pies
& more

crusts & toppings

A pie will never be truly perfect without a great piecrust and topping, so in this chapter I've included my favorite time-tested crust and topping recipes. I strongly urge you to make your own pie shell as opposed to using a store-bought version. It *will* take a bit more time and effort, but there's no question it's well worth it.

Of course, we begin with the basic Traditional Pastry Piecrust (page 4). I know that working with pastry pie dough can be intimidating, I promise you, though, it's not as challenging as you think. The trick to creating a truly amazing flaky, buttery piecrust is nothing more than correctly combining the right ingredients at the right temperature.

While everyone should have a traditional crust recipe in his or her arsenal, sometimes it's fun to mix it up with more unexpected variations. In this chapter, you'll find some great alternative crusts, such as Oreo Cookie Crust (page 10), Graham Cracker Crust (page 8), and even Pretzel Crust (page 11). Likewise, toppings are also a great way to create recipe variations and have some fun. This chapter includes a sweet, melt-in-your-mouth Cinnamon Sugar Crumb Topping (page 13), tropical Coconut Crumb Topping (page 13), and crunchy Walnut Crumb Topping (page 15).

Each pie recipe in this book will offer a standard crust and (if applicable) preferred topping choice. But always remember, these are just suggestions to get you started. I strongly encourage you to play around and swap out different crusts and toppings. It's an easy way to create a lot of variation in a single recipe.

Traditional Pastry Piecrust

Try this basic crust with Lattice Sour Cherry Pie (page 34), Maple Custard Pie (page 67), Peanut Butter Pie (page 93), Birthday Cake Surprise "Pie" (page 107), Open-Faced Apricot Raspberry Pie with an Apricot Glaze (page 23), Pumpkin Meringue Pie (page 49), and Turtle Pecan Pie (page 99).

Makes enough for one 9- or 10-inch double-crust piecrust

- 2 cups unbleached all-purpose flour
- 1 teaspoon salt
- ¾ cup plus 2 tablespoons Crisco, cold
- 5 tablespoons water, ice-cold
- ½ cup heavy cream

In a medium bowl, mix together the flour and salt. Add the Crisco to the flour mixture. Either with a pastry blender or with your fingertips, mix the ingredients together with an up-and-down chopping motion until the dough forms coarse, pea-size crumbs. Note: I prefer to use my fingertips, but take care not to overhandle the dough, because it will become difficult to work with; when dough is over-handled, the Crisco becomes *too* incorporated. In the perfect pie, the Crisco will have a marbleized look when the dough is rolled out, and you will actually be able to see Crisco swirls within the uncooked dough.

Add the ice-cold water, 1 tablespoon at a time, delicately incorporating each tablespoon into the flour mixture before you add the next. You may have to use 1 more or 1 less tablespoon of water than the amount recommended, depending upon the humidity in your kitchen at the time of baking. You will know you have added just the right amount of water when the dough forms a ball that easily holds together.

Use your palm to form the dough into a disk shape, wrap it with plastic, and place it in the refrigerator to chill for at least 30 minutes. Once the dough has chilled, divide the disk in half. You now have enough dough for either one 9- or 10-inch double-crust (1 pie shell and 1 top crust) or two 9- or 10-inch single crusts (pie shell only). If you are making a single-crust pie, you will use only one half of the dough per pie. Wrap the remaining half in plastic and reserve it in the refrigerator for future use; the dough can be reserved in the refrigerator for up to 5 days. Alternatively, you can make a second single-crust pie shell, wrap it tightly in plastic wrap, and freeze it for future use; it will keep for up to 1 month.

Preparing prebaked pie shells

A number of recipes in this book call for prebaked pie shells for the single-crust pies. Follow these directions before adding the desired filling.

Preheat the oven to 425°F.

To prepare the pie shell, divide the disk of dough in half, setting one half to the side. On a clean, lightly floured work surface, roll out the dough with a rolling pin until it forms a 10-inch circle. Fold the circle in half, place it in the pie plate so the edges of the circle drop over the rim, and unfold the dough to completely cover the pie plate. To crimp the pie dough, use your forefingers and thumbs. Press down with your forefingers and up with your thumbs to crimp the dough. Continue to crimp until the entire pie is completed. Brush heavy cream over the crimped edges to create a perfect, golden brown finish. Line the bottom of the crust with parchment paper and place pie weights on top to ensure the edges do not fall into the shell while the crust is baking. If you do not have pie weights, dried beans also work well.

To bake, place the pie plate on the middle rack of the oven and bake for 15 to 20 minutes, or until a golden brown color is achieved. Before removing the shell from the oven, make sure that the crust under the parchment paper has turned a golden brown.

Roll out the dough until about ⅛ inch thick. Make a circle about 10 inches in diameter for a regular piecrust and about 12 inches for a deep-dish pie.

Fold the dough circle in half so that it can easily be lifted and placed over the pie dish.

Unfold the dough until the dish is completely covered, then gently pat the dough into the pie dish so that it fits snugly. If dough tears, gently pinch together with fingertips.

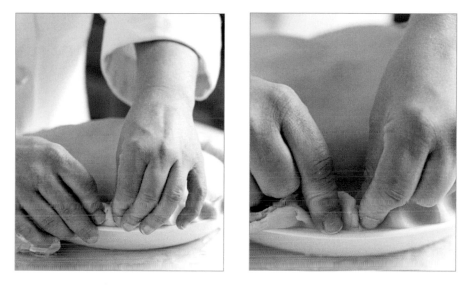

To crimp the pie dough, use your forefingers and thumbs. Press down with your forefingers and up with your thumbs to crimp the dough. Continue to crimp until the entire pie is completed.

Using Pie Weights

Pie weights keep the piecrust in place and stop air bubbles from forming when making prebaked shells. These small balls can be purchased in both metal and ceramic varieties or you can create your own makeshift pie weights by using dried beans. Cut a piece of parchment paper into a square shape and place it on top of the pie shell. Next, place the pie weights—distributing them evenly—on top of the parchment paper.

Graham Cracker Crust

Graham Cracker Crust is a great way to infuse sweetness and texture into a pie. Try this crust with Graham Cracker Cream Fluff Pie (page 65), White Chocolate Raspberry Swirl Pie (page 81), and Banoffee Pie (page 104).

Makes one 9-inch crust

24 graham cracker sheets, finely chopped (1½ cups)
 1 tablespoon sugar
 5 tablespoons unsalted butter, melted

Preheat the oven to 350°F.

In a food processor, pulsate the graham crackers until they are finely chopped. (If you do not have a food processor, you can also place the graham crackers in a plastic sandwich or freezer bag and roll over them with a rolling pin to crush the crackers into crumbs.) In a medium bowl, mix together the graham cracker crumbs and sugar. Add the melted butter, using your fingertips to incorporate it with the graham cracker mixture. Spread the graham cracker mixture evenly across the bottom and sides of a 9-inch pie plate and carefully pat flat so that it covers the entire dish. There should be no gaps in the crust.

Bake the crust for about 5 minutes, or until it's golden brown. Cool the pie shell for 30 minutes before adding your desired filling.

Graham Cracker Macadamia Coconut Crust

This bold crust packs in all the sweetness of Graham Cracker Crust (page 8), but with the addition of a coconut twist and even more crunch, thanks to the macadamia nuts. Turn Key Lime pie on its ear by using this unexpected crust for Lime Pie with Coconut Macadamia Crust (page 123) and Key Lime–Blackberry Chiffon Pie (page 119).

Makes one 9-inch crust

24 graham cracker sheets (1½ finely chopped cups)
 1 cup sweetened shredded coconut
½ cup unsalted macadamia nuts
 1 tablespoon sugar
 5 tablespoons unsalted butter, melted

In a food processor, pulsate the graham crackers, shredded coconut, macadamia nuts, and sugar until they are finely chopped and combined. Pour the ingredients into a medium bowl and incorporate the melted butter. Spread the mixture evenly across the bottom and sides of a 9-inch pie plate and carefully pat flat so that it covers the entire dish. There should be no gaps in the crust. Set the pie crust aside until you are ready to add your desired pie filling.

Oreo Cookie Crust

This crust pumps up the volume by providing a rich chocolate shell that will transform even the most basic filling into an out-of-this-world concoction. For an easy treat, just fill this crust with a basic chocolate or vanilla cream filling. Also be sure to try this with Almond Joy Pie (page 87) and Chocolate Silk Pie (page 63).

Makes one 9-inch crust

20 Oreo cookies

½ teaspoon ground cinnamon

2 tablespoons unsalted butter, melted

2 tablespoons whole milk

Preheat the oven to 350°F.

Place the Oreo cookies and cinnamon in a food processor and pulse them together until they are ground into fine crumbs. In a medium bowl, mix together the crumbs and melted butter, using a fork to combine. Add and incorporate the milk, ½ tablespoon at a time, stopping when the crumbs are moist enough to mold into a pie shell (this may take only 1½ tablespoons of milk to accomplish).

Spread the Oreo crust mixture evenly across the bottom and sides of a 9-inch pie plate and carefully pat flat so that it covers the entire dish. There should be no gaps in the crust. Bake for about 5 minutes, until slightly raised and firm. Cool the pie shell for 30 minutes before adding your desired pie filling.

Pretzel Crust

Pretzel Crust is about as untraditional as it gets, but I've found that this salty crust is a perfect complement to otherwise sweet pies. Try this with Candy Bar Pie (page 89).

Makes one 9-inch crust

- 2 cups pretzel sticks, chopped into fine pieces
- ¼ cup firmly packed dark brown sugar
- 8 tablespoons (1 stick) unsalted butter, melted

Preheat the oven to 350°F.

In a large bowl, mix together the chopped pretzels and brown sugar. Pour the melted butter over the dry ingredients and use your fingertips to combine all of the ingredients. Spread the pretzel mixture evenly across the bottom and sides of a 9-inch pie plate so that it covers the entire dish, with no gaps in the crust.

Place the piecrust in the oven and bake for about 10 minutes, or until the crust turns a golden brown. Remove the piecrust from the oven and allow it to cool before use.

Cinnamon Sugar Crumb Topping

This basic sweet crumb topping will absolutely melt in your mouth. Use this with any fruit pie if you prefer your treats on the sweeter side. Be sure to try it with Apple-Cranberry Pie (page 21), Mixed Berry Crumb Pie (page 26), Blueberry-Rhubarb Crumb Pie (page 30), Pear-Ginger Pie (page 42), and Blueberry Crumb Cake (page 184). Not only is this crumb topping a great pie topper, but it also works wonderfully atop crumb cakes and tea breads.

Makes enough topping for one 9-inch pie

½ cup unbleached all-purpose flour
⅓ cup firmly packed dark brown sugar
1 teaspoon ground cinnamon
¼ teaspoon salt
5 tablespoons unsalted butter, cold and cut into ¼-inch cubes

In a large bowl, mix together the flour, brown sugar, cinnamon, and salt. Using a pastry blender, incorporate the butter by cutting it into the flour until the butter forms small, pea-size pieces.

Pair the topping with a traditional pastry pie shell and the filling of your choice. Once the filling has been placed in the pie shell, sprinkle the cinnamon sugar crumb topping evenly over the filling until it is completely covered. Bake as directed.

Coconut Crumb Topping

Coconut Crumb Topping always catches people off guard and is an amazingly simple way to incorporate a tropical twist into your pies. This chewy crumb topping works great with summertime pies like Pineapple-Pomegranate Pie with a Coconut Crumb (page 44). If you want to get really creative, try this topping with Blueberry-Rhubarb Crumb Pie (page 30) or Mixed Berry Crumb Pie (page 26).

Makes enough topping for one 9-inch pie
½ cup unbleached all-purpose flour
⅓ cup firmly packed light brown sugar
1 teaspoon ground cinnamon
¼ teaspoon salt
½ cup sweetened shredded coconut
5 tablespoons unsalted butter, cold and cut into ¼-inch cubes

In a large bowl, mix together the flour, brown sugar, cinnamon, salt, and shredded coconut. Using a pastry blender, incorporate the butter by cutting it into the flour until the butter forms small, pea-size pieces.

Pair the topping with a traditional pastry pie shell and the filling of your choice. Once the filling has been placed in the pie shell, sprinkle the coconut crumb topping evenly over the filling until it is completely covered. Bake as directed.

Walnut Crumb Topping

Walnut Crumb Topping adds sustenance and texture to pies. If you're not a fan of walnuts, try substituting pecans, almonds, or your favorite nut (you can even do a nut mixture!). Try this with Pear-Ginger Pie (page 42), Black Plum Pie (page 46), and Cranberry Pie with Walnut Crumb (page 32).

Makes enough for one 9 inch pie

½ cup unbleached all-purpose flour

⅔ cup firmly packed light brown sugar

1½ teaspoons ground cinnamon

¼ teaspoon salt

5 tablespoons unsalted butter, cold and cut into ¼-inch cubes

¼ cup chopped walnuts

In a large bowl, combine the flour, brown sugar, cinnamon, and salt. Using a pastry blender, incorporate the butter by cutting it into the flour until the butter forms small, pea-size pieces. Add in the walnuts, using your fingers to gently incorporate them into the crumb base.

Pair this topping with a traditional pastry pie shell and the filling of your choice. Once the filling has been placed in the pie shell, distribute the walnut crumb topping evenly over the filling until it is completely covered. Bake as directed.

fruit pies

Whether it's apple or strawberry, pumpkin or peach, most of us have a go-to fruit pie: pumpkin pie for Thanksgiving, Grandma's apple pie in the fall, peach pie in the summer. I love the ability of those tastes and smells to transport us back to the kitchens of people we love and special times in our past.

Now, having said all of that, it's also easy to get stuck in a pie rut and miss out on some sumptuous and exciting flavor combinations—and maybe even a few *new* traditions! There are so many possibilities with fruit pies that it's a shame to *only* indulge in the tried and true.

This chapter is chock-full of fruit pies that are a little outside the expected and traditional. The flavors themselves won't be new to you, but incorporating them in these unique ways may very well be. Both peach and strawberry pies are favorite summertime delights—but what about mixing the two together in a sweet and satisfying Peach-Strawberry Crumb Pie (page 38)? Venture way outside of the box and give Pineapple-Pomegranate Pie with a Coconut Crumb (page 44) a whirl. It's also fun to experiment a little with common pie types. Make apple pie even richer with Apple Caramel Crunch Pie (page 18) and mix up this year's Thanksgiving pumpkin pie by adding a beautiful meringue crown for Pumpkin Meringue Pie (page 49).

Fruit pies—and especially the sugar-free fruit pies—are always at their best when using fresh fruit. Using seasonal ingredients is also a great way to ensure that you're rotating pies throughout the year, rather than having the same pie over and over again.

Apple Caramel Crunch Pie

I like to make Apple Caramel Crunch Pie at the height of the autumn harvest because its Heath toffee bar pieces are the culinary equivalent of that satisfying crunch of stepping on newly fallen leaves. With caramel sauce drizzled over the sweet topping and infused in the apple-pecan filling, this pie is somewhat reminiscent of a caramel apple. I prefer to use Cortland, but Granny Smith, Crispin, Northern Spy, or Empire apples also work well. I have included my favorite recipe for Caramel Sauce (page 222), but if you're looking to save some time, feel free to use store-bought caramel sauce instead.

Makes one 9-inch pie, 6 to 8 slices
Level: Moderate

Crust and Topping

1   recipe Traditional Pastry Piecrust dough for a 9-inch single-crust pie (page 4)

¼   cup heavy cream (to glaze the crimped pie edges)

Cinnamon Sugar Crumb Topping (page 13)

½   cup coarsely chopped pieces of Heath toffee bar

Filling

1   cup chopped pecans

¾   cup sugar

2   tablespoons unbleached all-purpose flour

1   tablespoon ground cinnamon

Dash of ground nutmeg

8   medium apples, peeled, cored, and cut into ½-inch chunks

1   cup Caramel Sauce (page 222)

Preheat the oven to 350°F. Line a baking sheet with parchment paper and set aside.

To prepare the pie shell, on a clean, lightly floured work surface, roll out half the disk of dough with a rolling pin until it forms a 10-inch circle. Wrap the remaining half of the dough tightly in plastic wrap and reserve it in the refrigerator for future use for up to 5 days. Fold the circle in half, place it in a 9-inch pie plate so that the edges of the circle drop over the rim, and unfold the dough to completely cover the pie plate. Using your thumb and index finger, crimp the edges of the pie shell. Brush the edges of the pie shell with heavy cream to create a perfect, golden brown finish. Set the pie shell to the side while you make the filling.

Place the pecans on a baking sheet and bake them for about 5 minutes, or until they are lightly toasted. Remove the pecans from the oven and raise the temperature to 425°F to preheat for the pie.

While the pecans are toasting, begin making the filling. In a small bowl, whisk together the sugar, flour, cinnamon, and nutmeg. Place the apple chunks in a large bowl and toss them with the sugar mixture, thoroughly coating them. When the toasted pecans have cooled, put them in the apples and toss thoroughly. Pour ½ cup of the caramel sauce on the bottom of the unbaked pie shell and spread it evenly across (reserve the rest of the sauce for the garnish). Place the apple mixture on top of the caramel. Add the Heath toffee bar pieces to the cinnamon sugar crumb topping, then sprinkle the crumb topping over the apple filling, covering it completely.

To bake, place the pie plate on the lined baking sheet and bake it for 15 minutes. Reduce the heat to 375°F and continue baking for about 40 minutes more, or until the crust is golden brown and the apples are tender. Insert a cake tester or a knife into the pie to check the firmness of the apples. Transfer the pie plate to a wire cooling rack and allow the pie to cool and set for 1½ hours before serving. Once the pie has completely cooled, drizzle the remaining ½ cup of caramel sauce over the crumb topping.

Apple Caramel Crunch Pie is best served at room temperature or warmed at 350°F for about 10 minutes. It will keep at room temperature overnight and can be stored in the refrigerator for up to 4 days.

Apple-Cranberry Pie

The combination of fresh cranberries and apples results in a colorful pie that incorporates all of those wonderful, warm-you-up-from-the-inside flavors we love to indulge in during the harvest and holiday months. Fresh lemon juice and orange zest add an unexpected citrus twist to the apple flavor. I like to use Cortland apples for this pie, but Ida Reds, Crispins, Northern Spy, Granny Smith, or your preferred baking apple will work, too. If you would like to add a sweet touch to counterbalance the tartness of the cranberry, try this pie with a crumb topping of your choice.

Makes one 9-inch pie, 6 to 8 slices
Level: Moderate

Crust

1   recipe Traditional Pastry Piecrust dough for a 9-inch double-crust pie (page 4)
¼   cup heavy cream (to glaze the top of the pie)

Filling

8   cups apples (4 to 5 medium apples), peeled, cored, and cut into ½-inch chunks
2   tablespoons fresh lemon juice
½   tablespoon grated orange zest
1   cup sugar
⅓   cup unbleached all-purpose flour
1   tablespoon ground cinnamon
    Dash of ground nutmeg
1   cup fresh whole cranberries, washed and dried
1   tablespoon salted butter

Preheat the oven to 425°F. Line a baking sheet with parchment paper and set aside.

To prepare the pie shell, on a clean, lightly floured work surface, roll out half the disk of dough with a rolling pin until it forms a 10-inch circle. Set the remaining half of the dough aside to use as the pie top after you have completed the filling. Fold the circle in half, place it in a 9-inch pie plate so that the edges of the circle drop over the rim, and unfold the dough to completely cover the pie plate. Set the pie shell to the side while you make the filling.

To prepare the filling, in a medium bowl, toss together the apples, lemon juice, and orange zest. Set the mixture aside. In a small bowl, whisk together the sugar, flour, cinnamon, and nutmeg. Sprinkle this dry mixture over the apples and toss to completely combine. Add the cranberries and continue to toss until all of the ingredients are well combined. Place the apple-cranberry mixture in the bottom of the pie shell. Dot the fruit with the butter.

To prepare the top crust, roll out the second half of the dough with a rolling pin until it forms a 10-inch circle. Fold the dough circle in half and place it over the filling, with the straight line of the half circle running down the middle of the pie. Unfold the circle so that the entire pie is covered. Using your thumb and index finger, crimp the edges of the pie together to seal in the filling. Puncture the top of the pie with a fork to allow ventilation and brush the top of the pie with the heavy cream to achieve a golden brown crust.

To bake, place the pie plate on the lined baking sheet on the middle rack of the oven and bake it for 15 minutes. Reduce the heat to 350°F and continue baking for 40 to 45 minutes more, or until the crust is golden brown, the apples are tender, and the juices are bubbling. Insert a cake tester or a knife into the pie to check the firmness of the apples. Transfer the pie plate to a wire cooling rack and allow the pie to cool and set for 1½ hours before serving.

Apple-Cranberry Pie can be stored at room temperature for up to 3 days or in the refrigerator for 4 days.

Open-Faced Apricot-Raspberry Pie with an Apricot Glaze

I live for that split second when someone bites into one of my pies and a totally unexpected flavor bursts to life in his or her mouth. This light apricot-raspberry pie dripping with fruit flavor is a surefire way to get that reaction. This pie is the perfect finish to a heavy barbecue dinner or as the final note of a light lunch. The individual steps of this recipe are relatively simple, but plan ahead to be sure you allot enough preparation time since a few separate steps are required. Note that the final step (making the apricot glaze) should be completed right before serving.

Makes one 9-inch pie, 6 to 8 slices
Level: Moderate

Crust
1 prebaked 9-inch Traditional Pastry Piecrust shell (page 4)

Apricot Filling
½ vanilla bean, halved lengthwise, seeds scraped out with the tip of a sharp knife, seeds and pod reserved

1½ cups water

1¼ cups granulated sugar

½ teaspoon grated lemon zest

1½ pounds pitted apricots, with the skin on, cut into ½-inch slices

Cream Cheese Filling
3 ounces cream cheese, softened

½ cup confectioners' sugar

¾ cup heavy cream

½ cup fresh raspberries, washed and dried

Apricot Glaze

10 ounces apricot jam

¼ cup water

2 tablespoons Grand Marnier

To prepare the apricot filling, place the vanilla bean seeds, the reserved pod, the water, granulated sugar, and lemon zest in a medium saucepan off of the heat and mix well. Turn the heat to high and bring the ingredients to a boil for 1 minute. Once the mixture is boiling, carefully add the apricots. Stir occasionally as the mixture boils for about 5 minutes more, or until the apricots are tender. Transfer the apricots and liquid to a medium bowl and allow them to cool completely. Discard the vanilla pod.

Vanilla Beans vs. Vanilla Extract

Bakers have different preferences when it comes to choosing between vanilla beans and pure vanilla extract. Although using vanilla beans requires a bit more effort, I generally prefer using them because I believe they provide a richer, more pronounced vanilla flavor. I also like the visual effect of the vanilla seeds—those little black specks you've probably noticed in crème brûlée or high-quality vanilla ice cream. Most grocery stores carry vanilla beans in their spice section. The beans can easily dry out, so make sure to keep the storage container closed tightly between uses.

Once the apricots have cooled, begin preparing the cream cheese filling. Using an electric mixer set on high speed, beat the cream cheese until it's smooth. Scrape the cream cheese off the sides of the bowl, then add the confectioners' sugar and heavy cream. Beat the ingredients on high speed until you have achieved a thick consistency that is able to hold its form.

Spread the cream cheese filling evenly across the bottom of the pie shell. Drain the liquid from the apricot filling and place the apricots neatly on top of the cream cheese filling, distributing them evenly across. Arrange the raspberries neatly on top of the apricots. Place the pie in the refrigerator for at least 2 hours, or until you are ready to glaze it (right before serving).

To prepare the apricot glaze, place the apricot jam, water, and Grand Marnier in a small saucepan off of the heat and mix well. Place the saucepan over high heat and bring the ingredients to a boil until the jam dissolves, 3 to 5 minutes. Take the saucepan off of the heat and allow the glaze to cool for 5 minutes. With a pastry brush, glaze the top of the apricots and raspberries to give the pie a perfect shine.

Open-Faced Apricot Raspberry Pie should be served cold. It can be stored in the refrigerator for up to 2 days.

Mixed Berry Crumb Pie

While all of these berries make a scrumptious dessert in and of themselves, combined they meld into a delicious combination of tart and sweet, topped off with a melt-in-your-mouth crumb topping. Who says you can't have it all? If you prefer your pie a little less sweet, try this with a Traditional Pastry Piecrust double crust (page 4) or, for a little extra crunch, give Walnut Crumb Topping (page 15) a whirl. Whatever topping you choose, Mixed Berry Crumb Pie goes great with a scoop of vanilla ice cream.

Makes one 9-inch pie, 6 to 8 slices
Level: Easy

Crust and Topping

1   recipe Traditional Pastry Piecrust dough for a 9-inch single-crust pie (page 4)
¼   cup heavy cream (to glaze the crimped pie edges)
    Cinnamon Sugar Crumb Topping (page 13)

Filling

1   cup sugar
½   cup unbleached all-purpose flour
½   teaspoon ground cinnamon
1   cup blackberries
1   cup raspberries
1   cup blueberries
1   cup hulled and quartered strawberries

Preheat the oven to 425°F. Line a baking sheet with parchment paper and set aside.

To prepare the pie shell, on a clean, lightly floured work surface, roll out half the

disk of dough with a rolling pin until it forms a 10-inch circle. Wrap the remaining half of the dough tightly in plastic wrap and reserve it in the refrigerator for future use for up to 5 days. Fold the circle in half, place it in a 9-inch pie plate so that the edges of the circle drop over the rim, and unfold the dough to completely cover the pie plate. Using your thumb and index finger, crimp the edges of the pie shell. Brush the edges of the pie shell with heavy cream to create a perfect, golden brown finish. Set the pie shell to the side while you make the filling.

To prepare the filling, in a small bowl, whisk together the sugar, flour, and cinnamon. Wash and dry all of the berries thoroughly. Place the berries in a large bowl and sprinkle them with the sugar mixture, gently spreading it throughout, making sure that all of the berries are evenly coated. Place the berries evenly along the bottom of the unbaked pie shell. Sprinkle the crumb topping over the berry filling, covering it completely.

To bake, place the pie plate on the lined baking sheet and bake it for 15 minutes. Reduce the heat to 375°F and continue baking for about 40 minutes, or until the crust is golden brown and the juices are bubbling. Transfer the pie plate to a wire cooling rack and allow the pie to cool and set for 1½ hours before serving.

Mixed Berry Crumb Pie is best served at room temperature or warmed at 350°F for about 10 minutes. It will keep at room temperature overnight and can be stored in the refrigerator for up to 4 days.

Blueberry-Cherry Sugar-Free Pie

It's very important to me that Michele's Pies provide options for customers who are watching their sugar intake. It's also important to me that my sugar-free offerings be just as tasty as every other pie in my shop. When making any sugar-free pie, it's always best to use the ripest fruits possible to help counteract the lack of additional sugars. *Especially* when using fresh blueberries and cherries, it's almost impossible to taste the difference between this pie and its sugary counterpart. If you'd like to try this pie with sugar, just substitute 1 cup of sugar for the Splenda.

Makes one 9-inch pie, 6 to 8 slices
Level: Moderate

Crust and Topping
1 recipe Traditional Pastry Piecrust dough for a 9-inch double-crust pie (page 4)
¼ cup heavy cream (to glaze the crimped pie edges and the top of the pie)

Filling
¾ cup Splenda
¼ cup unbleached all-purpose flour
½ teaspoon salt
1 teaspoon ground cinnamon
2½ cups cherries (preferably Rainier), stemmed, pitted, and cut in half
2½ cups blueberries, rinsed and dried
1 tablespoon fresh lemon juice
1 tablespoon unsalted butter

Preheat the oven to 425°F. Line a baking sheet with parchment paper and set aside.

To prepare the pie shell, on a clean, lightly floured work surface, roll out half the

disk of dough with a rolling pin until it forms a 10-inch circle. Set the remaining half of dough aside to use as the pie top after you have completed the filling. Fold the circle in half, place it in a 9-inch pie plate so that the edges of the circle drop over the rim, and unfold the dough to completely cover the pie plate. Set the pie shell aside while you prepare the filling.

To prepare the filling, in a small bowl, whisk together the Splenda, flour, salt, and cinnamon. In a medium bowl, toss together the cherries and blueberries. Sprinkle the lemon juice over the fruit and gently toss to evenly coat the cherries and blueberries. Sprinkle the dry ingredients over the fruit and gently toss again so that all ingredients are well combined. Spoon the fruit into the pie shell, spreading it evenly across the bottom. Dot the filling with the butter.

To prepare the top crust, roll out the second half of the dough with a rolling pin until it forms a 10-inch circle. Fold the dough circle in half and place it over the filling, with the straight line of the half circle running down the middle of the pie. Unfold the circle so that the entire pie is covered. Using your thumb and index finger, crimp the edges of the pie together to seal in the filling, and then use a fork to puncture the top of the pie 5 or 6 times to allow for ventilation. Brush the top of the pie and the crimped edges with heavy cream to create a perfect, golden brown finish.

To bake, place the pie plate on the lined baking sheet and bake it for 15 minutes. Reduce the heat to 350°F and continue baking for about 40 minutes more, or until the crust is golden brown and the juices are bubbling over the side of the pie. Transfer the pie plate to a wire cooling rack and allow the pie to cool and set for 1½ hours before serving.

Blueberry-Cherry Sugar-Free Pie is best served at room temperature or warmed at 350°F for about 10 minutes. It will keep at room temperature overnight and can be stored in the refrigerator for up to 3 days.

Blueberry-Rhubarb Crumb Pie

Quick! What's the first thing you think of when you hear the word *rhubarb*? I'm willing to bet that, for most, it's "strawberry," right? While strawberry-rhubarb is definitely the pie world's version of peanut butter and jelly, believe it or not, blueberry-rhubarb is equally good and will send your taste buds into overdrive. This recipe uses a sweet crumb topping that offsets the rhubarb's tartness; however, if you want to really savor that tart taste, try this with a Traditional Pastry Piecrust double crust (page 4).

Makes one 9-inch pie, 6 to 8 slices
Level: Easy

Crust and Topping

1 recipe Traditional Pastry Piecrust dough for a 9-inch single-crust pie (page 4)

¼ cup heavy cream (to glaze the crimped pie edges)

Cinnamon Sugar Crumb Topping (page 13)

Filling

2 cups blueberries, washed and dried

1 cup sugar

¼ cup unbleached all-purpose flour

½ teaspoon ground cinnamon

4 to 5 stalks rhubarb, trimmed and sliced into ½-inch-thick chunks (2 cups)

1 tablespoon cornstarch

1 tablespoon quick-cooking tapioca

Preheat the oven to 400°F. Line a baking sheet with parchment paper and set aside.

To prepare the pie shell, on a clean, lightly floured work surface, roll out half the

disk of dough with a rolling pin until it forms a 10-inch circle. Wrap the remaining half of the dough tightly in plastic wrap and reserve it in the refrigerator for future use for up to 5 days. Fold the circle in half, place it in a 9-inch pie plate so that the edges of the circle drop over the rim, and unfold the dough to completely cover the pie plate. Using your thumb and index finger, crimp the edges of the pie shell. Brush the edges of the pie shell with heavy cream to create a perfect, golden brown finish. Set the pie shell to the side while you make the filling.

To prepare the filling, place the blueberries in a medium bowl. In a separate medium bowl, whisk together ½ cup of the sugar, the flour, and the cinnamon. Pour the dry ingredient mixture over the blueberries. Gently toss until the blueberries are evenly coated.

In a separate medium bowl, toss the rhubarb with the remaining ½ cup sugar, the cornstarch, and the tapioca until the rhubarb is evenly coated. Combine the rhubarb and blueberries in a single bowl and gently toss until they are well combined. Place the blueberry-rhubarb filling in the pie shell, spreading it evenly across the bottom. Sprinkle the crumb topping over the berry filling, covering it completely.

To bake, place the pie plate on the lined baking sheet and bake it for 15 minutes. Reduce the heat to 350°F and continue baking for about 40 minutes more, or until the crust is golden brown and the juices are bubbling. Transfer the pie plate to a wire cooling rack and allow the pie to cool and set for 1½ hours before serving.

Blueberry-Rhubarb Crumb Pie is best served at room temperature or warmed at 350°F for about 10 minutes. It will keep at room temperature overnight and can be stored in the refrigerator for up to 4 days.

Cranberry Pie with Walnut Crumb

When making this pie, I always opt for fresh cranberries, but this fruit *does* have a short season. If you want to enjoy cranberry pie out of season, feel free to try frozen cranberries; just make sure they are thawed properly before you begin. Walnut crumb is my topping of choice here because it gives this pie an extra bit of crunch. However, if you really want to maximize tartness, try this recipe with a Traditional Pastry Piecrust double crust (page 4). Add a scoop of vanilla ice cream on top to cut some of the tartness.

Makes one 9-inch pie, 6 to 8 slices
Level: Easy

Crust and Topping

1 recipe Traditional Pastry Piecrust dough for a 9-inch single-crust pie (page 4)

¼ cup heavy cream (to glaze the crimped pie edges)

2 cups Walnut Crumb Topping (page 15)

Filling

3 eggs, slightly beaten

1 cup sugar

½ cup light corn syrup

1 tablespoon butter, melted

½ teaspoon salt

12 ounces fresh cranberries, washed, dried, and coarsely chopped in a food processor

Preheat the oven to 375°F. Line a baking sheet with parchment paper and set aside.

To prepare the pie shell, on a clean, lightly floured work surface, roll out half the

disk of dough with a rolling pin until it forms a 10-inch circle. Wrap the remaining half of the dough tightly in plastic wrap and reserve it in the refrigerator for future use for up to 5 days. Fold the circle in half, place it in a 9-inch pie plate so that the edges of the circle drop over the rim, and unfold the dough to completely cover the pie plate. Using your thumb and index finger, crimp the edges of the pie shell. Brush the edges of the pie shell with heavy cream to create a perfect, golden brown finish. Set the pie shell to the side while you make the filling.

To prepare the filling, using an electric mixer set at medium speed, mix together the eggs, sugar, corn syrup, melted butter, and salt. Once the ingredients are blended, fold the cranberries in. Pour the filling into the pie shell, spreading it evenly across the bottom. Sprinkle the walnut crumb topping over the cranberry filling, covering it completely.

To bake, place the pie plate on the lined baking sheet and bake it for 15 minutes. Reduce the heat to 350°F and continue baking for 35 to 40 minutes more, or until the crust is golden brown and the juices are bubbling. Transfer the pie plate to a wire cooling rack and allow the pie to cool for 30 to 60 minutes before serving.

Cranberry Pie with Walnut Crumb can be served at room temperature or warmed at 350°F for about 10 minutes. It will keep at room temperature overnight and can be stored in the refrigerator for up to 3 days.

Lattice Sour Cherry Pie

This sour cherry version of the classic packs an unexpected tartness that will really wake up your taste buds. Here in New England, sour cherries have a very short season, so I like to take advantage of these when I can. (Depending on your location, sour cherries are typically in season from late summer into early fall.) The lattice top here allows the colors and juices of the cherries to peek through, making the final result delicious *and* beautiful. Note that this pie should cool for at least 3 hours before serving, so plan accordingly.

Makes one 9-inch pie, 6 to 8 slices
Level: Moderate

Crust

1 recipe Traditional Pastry Piecrust dough (page 4) for a 9-inch double-crust pie (half of the dough will be used for the pie shell and half will be used for the lattice topping)

¼ cup heavy cream (to glaze the crimped pie edges and the lattice top)

Filling

1 cup sugar

¼ teaspoon salt

4 tablespoons cornstarch

5 cups sour cherries, stemmed and pitted

1 tablespoon fresh lemon juice

1 teaspoon pure vanilla extract

Preheat the oven to 425°F. Line a baking sheet with parchment paper and set aside.

To prepare the pie shell, on a clean, lightly floured work surface, roll out half the

disk of dough with a rolling pin until it forms a 10-inch circle. Set the remaining half of dough aside to use for the lattice topping after you have completed the filling. Fold the circle in half, place it in a 9-inch pie plate so that the edges of the circle drop over the rim, and unfold the dough to completely cover the pie plate. Using your thumb and index finger, crimp the edges of the pie shell. Set the pie shell to the side while you make the filling.

To prepare the filling, in a medium bowl, whisk together the sugar, salt, and cornstarch. Add the sour cherries, tossing gently to combine the fruit and dry ingredients. Make sure that all of the cherries are evenly coated. Stir in the lemon juice and vanilla. Place the cherry mixture in the pie shell, distributing it evenly.

To assemble the lattice crust, roll out the second half of the dough to about ¼-inch thickness. Using a sharp knife or a pastry wheel, cut the round into ¾-inch-wide strips. Place the strips over the top of the pie filling, lattice style, so that the edges of the strips meet the crimped edges of the pie shell. Ultimately, you want to create a checkerboard effect, with the lattice strips placed both vertically and horizontally across the pie, weaving the dough strips in and out so that there is an over-under pattern. Trim the edges of the extra dough hanging over the pie plate and work the rough edges into the crimped edges of the crust. Brush the edges of the pie shell and the lattice top with heavy cream to create a perfect, golden brown finish.

To bake, place the pie plate on the lined baking sheet and bake it for 15 minutes. Reduce the heat to 375°F and continue baking for 40 to 45 minutes more, or until the crust is golden brown and the juices are bubbling. Transfer the pie plate to a wire cooling rack and allow the pie to cool and set for 3 hours before serving. This pie goes great with a scoop of vanilla ice cream.

Lattice Sour Cherry Pie is best served at room temperature or warmed at 350°F for about 10 minutes. It will keep at room temperature overnight and can be stored in the refrigerator for up to 3 days.

Lemon Chess Pie

Seeing as how chess pie is a Southern classic, it's no surprise that this lemon version is a wonderful accompaniment to a hot summer's day. The traditional roots of this thick, custardy pie are evident in the ingredient list: You'll notice it consists of just a few simple ingredients that would have been easy to procure in the region's more agrarian days. Another defining feature is that, unlike most custard pies, chess pies call for a bit of cornmeal for a slightly denser filling.

Makes one 9-inch pie, 8 slices
Level: Easy

Crust

1   recipe Traditional Pastry Piecrust dough for a 9-inch single-crust pie (page 4)
¼   cup heavy cream (to glaze the crimped pie edges)

Filling

4   eggs
2   cups sugar
⅓   cup fresh lemon juice
4   tablespoons (½ stick) unsalted butter, melted
¼   cup heavy cream
¼   cup whole milk
2   tablespoons grated lemon zest
1   tablespoon unbleached all-purpose flour
1   tablespoon yellow cornmeal

Preheat the oven to 350°F. Line a baking sheet with parchment paper and set aside.

To prepare the pie shell, on a clean, lightly floured work surface, roll out half the

disk of dough with a rolling pin until it forms a 10-inch circle. Wrap the remaining half of the dough tightly in plastic wrap and reserve it in the refrigerator for future use for up to 5 days. Fold the circle in half, place it in a 9-inch pie plate so that the edges of the circle drop over the rim, and unfold the dough to completely cover the pie plate. Using your thumb and index finger, crimp the edges of the pie shell. Brush the edges of the pie shell with heavy cream to create a perfect, golden brown finish. Set the pie shell to the side while you make the filling.

To prepare the filling, using an electric mixer set on high speed, beat the eggs until they are foamy. Lower the speed to medium and add the sugar, lemon juice, melted butter, heavy cream, milk, lemon zest, flour, and cornmeal. Continue mixing until all of the ingredients are well combined, scraping the sides of the bowl at least twice. Pour the lemon mixture into the unbaked pie shell, spreading it evenly across the bottom.

To bake, place the pie plate on the lined baking sheet and bake it for about 50 minutes, or until it's firm in the middle but still soft to the touch. Transfer the pie plate to a wire cooling rack and allow the pie to cool and set for at least 3 hours before serving.

Lemon Chess Pie should be served cold. It can be stored in the refrigerator for up to 3 days.

Peach-Strawberry Crumb Pie

Peach pie is easily one of my shop's most anticipated summertime fruit pies. Every year, excited customers come into the store looking for it weeks before we even receive our first batch of peaches. As a treat for dedicated peach pie fans, I created this little twist on a favorite, adding strawberries—another summertime staple—to the mix. The crumb topping adds even more sweetness to this concoction; however, if you would prefer a little less sweetness, this pie also works great with a Traditional Pastry Piecrust double crust (page 4).

Makes one 9-inch pie, 6 to 8 slices
Level: Easy

Crust and Topping
1   recipe Traditional Pastry Piecrust dough for a 9-inch single-crust pie (page 4)
¼   cup heavy cream (to glaze the crimped pie edges)
    Cinnamon Sugar Crumb Topping (page 13)

Filling
¾   cup sugar
2   tablespoons cornstarch
2   tablespoons quick-cooking tapioca
1   teaspoon ground cinnamon
    Pinch of salt
4   cups sliced peaches (6 to 8 peaches, peeled, pitted, and cut into ½-inch slices)
2   cups hulled and quartered strawberries

Preheat the oven to 375°F. Line a baking sheet with parchment paper and set aside.

To prepare the pie shell, on a clean, lightly floured work surface, roll out half the disk of dough with a rolling pin until it forms a 10-inch circle. Wrap the remaining half of the dough tightly in plastic wrap and reserve it in the refrigerator for future use for up to 5 days. Fold the circle in half, place it in a 9-inch pie plate so that the edges of the circle drop over the rim, and unfold the dough to completely cover the pie plate. Using your thumb and index finger, crimp the edges of the pie shell. Brush the edges of the pie shell with heavy cream to create a perfect, golden brown finish. Set the pie shell to the side while you make the filling.

To prepare the filling, in a small bowl, whisk together the sugar, cornstarch, tapioca, cinnamon, and salt. In a medium bowl, gently toss together the peaches and strawberries. Pour the sugar mixture over the peaches and strawberries, tossing gently until they are well combined. Place the peach-strawberry filling in the pie shell, distributing it evenly. Sprinkle the crumb topping over the filling, covering it completely.

To bake, place the pie plate on the lined baking sheet and bake it for 50 to 55 minutes, or until the crust and topping are golden brown and the fruit is tender as tested by the point of a sharp knife. Transfer the pie plate to a wire cooling rack and allow the pie to cool and set for 1½ hours before serving.

Peach-Strawberry Crumb Pie is best served at room temperature or warmed at 350°F for about 10 minutes. It will keep at room temperature overnight and can be stored in the refrigerator for up to 4 days.

Peaches & Cream Pie

What more do you need than a sweet sugar-cinnamon topping melting right into a creamy peach filling? This recipe really goes into orbit when made with the ripest summer peaches available. If you have a barbecue cookout on your summer agenda, this should definitely be on the menu.

Makes one 9-inch pie, 6 to 8 slices
Level: Easy

Crust

1   recipe Traditional Pastry Piecrust dough for a 9-inch single-crust pie (page 4)

¼   cup heavy cream (to glaze the crimped pie edges)
    Cinnamon Sugar Crumb Topping (page 13)

Filling

2   tablespoons unbleached all-purpose flour

¾   cup sugar

¼   teaspoon salt

¼   cup sour cream

½   cup heavy cream

1   egg, beaten

½   teaspoon pure vanilla extract

2   cups sliced peaches (3 to 4 peaches peeled, pitted, and cut into ½-inch slices (see page 41)

Preheat the oven to 400°F. Line a baking sheet with parchment paper and set aside.

To prepare the pie shell, on a clean, lightly floured work surface, roll out half the

disk of dough with a rolling pin until it forms a 10-inch circle. Wrap the remaining half of the dough tightly in plastic wrap and reserve it in the refrigerator for future use for up to 5 days. Fold the circle in half, place it in a 9-inch pie plate so that the edges of the circle drop over the rim, and unfold the dough to completely cover the pie plate. Using your thumb and index finger, crimp the edges of the pie shell. Brush the edges of the pie shell with heavy cream to create a perfect, golden brown finish. Set the pie shell to the side while you make the filling.

How to Peel a Peach

Fill a medium saucepan with enough water to fully immerse the peaches and bring it to a boil. Using a sharp knife, cut a shallow X on the bottom of the peaches. Fill a medium bowl with ice-cold water and set it to the side. Once the water has reached a boil, place the peaches in the boiling water for 30 seconds. Remove the peaches from the saucepan and immediately place them in the bowl of cold water. Once the peaches have cooled, start peeling off the skin at the X and then halve, pit, and slice into wedges.

To prepare the filling, using an electric mixer on medium speed, combine the flour, sugar, salt, sour cream, heavy cream, beaten egg, and vanilla. Continue mixing until the ingredients are well combined.

Arrange the peach slices across the bottom of the unbaked pie shell. Pour the sour cream mixture over the peaches, distributing it evenly.

To bake, place the pie plate on the lined baking sheet and bake it for 15 minutes. Reduce the heat to 350°F and continue baking for 20 minutes more. Remove the pie from the oven and carefully sprinkle the crumb topping over the top of the pie. Place the pie back in the oven and continue baking for about 25 minutes, or until the crumb topping is golden brown and the pie is firm in the middle but still soft to the touch. Remove the pie from the oven and allow it to cool for about 15 minutes before serving.

Peaches & Cream Pie is best served at room temperature or warmed at 350°F for about 10 minutes. This pie can be stored in the refrigerator for up to 4 days.

Pear-Ginger Pie

Pears are one of my very favorite fall and winter fruits—especially when they're ripe and juicy. I prefer to use Bartlett pears for baking, but if you prefer another variety, feel free to try it in this recipe. The ginger in this recipe is quite pronounced, so if you're a fan of this spicy flavor, you will really love this pie. I've used a traditional double crust in this recipe, but it also works great with a Cinnamon Sugar Crumb Topping (page 13).

Makes one 9-inch pie, 6 to 8 slices
Level: Easy

Crust and Topping

1   recipe Traditional Pastry Piecrust dough for a 9-inch double-crust pie (page 4)

¼   cup heavy cream (to glaze the crimped pie edges and the top of the pie)

Filling

6   cups cubed ripe pears (6 to 8 ripe pears, peeled, cored, and cut into ½-inch cubes)

½   cup sugar

⅛   cup Grade B pure Vermont maple syrup (Grade A will also work)

2½   tablespoons quick-cooking tapioca

1   tablespoon fresh lemon juice

1   teaspoon pure vanilla extract

½   teaspoon ground ginger

1   tablespoon salted butter

Preheat the oven to 425°F. Line a baking sheet with parchment paper and set aside.

To prepare the pie shell, on a clean, lightly floured work surface, roll out half the

disk of dough with a rolling pin until it forms a 10-inch circle. Set the remaining half of dough aside to use as the pie top after you have completed the filling. Fold the circle in half, place it in a 9-inch pie plate so that the edges of the circle drop over the rim, and unfold the dough to completely cover the pie plate. Set the pie shell to the side while you make the filling.

To prepare the filling, in a medium bowl, combine the pears, sugar, maple syrup, tapioca, lemon juice, vanilla, and ginger. Toss until all of the ingredients are thoroughly combined. Place the filling in the pie shell, spreading it evenly across. Dot the filling with the butter.

To prepare the top crust, roll out the second half of the dough with a rolling pin until it forms a 10-inch circle. Fold the dough circle in half and place it over the filling, with the straight line of the half circle running down the middle of the pie. Unfold the circle so that the entire pie is covered. Using your thumb and index finger, crimp the edges of the pie together to seal in the filling, and then use a fork to puncture the top of the pie 5 or 6 times to allow ventilation. Brush the top of the pie and the crimped edges with heavy cream to create a perfect, golden brown finish.

To bake, place the pie plate on the lined baking sheet and bake it for 15 minutes. Reduce the heat to 350°F and continue baking for 35 to 40 minutes more, or until the pie juices are bubbling and the crust is golden brown. Transfer the pie plate to a wire cooling rack and allow the pie to cool and set for 1½ hours before serving.

Pear-Ginger Pie is best served at room temperature or warmed at 350°F for about 10 minutes. It will keep at room temperature overnight and can be stored in the refrigerator for up to 4 days.

Pineapple-Pomegranate Pie with a Coconut Crumb

Pineapple and pomegranate are an admittedly atypical combination. Melding these two fruits together probably wouldn't have occurred to me without some prompting; the idea for this offbeat combination actually came from some children of close family friends. I thought they might be on to something, although I wasn't sure what to expect when I made this pie for the first time. It turns out that, when combined, the pineapple flavor takes center stage, with the pomegranate seeds adding a burst of color and pleasing texture. A little more refining taught me that this pie is at its tastiest with a coconut crumb topping, which really complements the pineapple and pomegranate. If you're not a fan of coconut, Cinnamon Sugar Crumb Topping (page 13) also works well with this pie.

Makes one 9-inch pie, 6 to 8 slices
Level: Easy

Crust

1 recipe Traditional Pastry Piecrust dough for a 9-inch single-crust pie (page 4)

¼ cup heavy cream (to glaze the crimped pie edges)
   Coconut Crumb Topping (page 14)

Filling

6 cups fresh cubed pineapple (from about 1 pineapple, trimmed and cut into ½-inch cubes)

1 cup pomegranate seeds

1 cup sugar

1 teaspoon ground cinnamon

1 tablespoon salted butter

Preheat the oven to 425°F. Line a baking sheet with parchment paper and set aside.

To prepare the pie shell, on a clean, lightly floured work surface, roll out half the disk of dough with a rolling pin until it forms a 10-inch circle. Wrap the remaining half of the dough tightly in plastic wrap and reserve it in the refrigerator for future use for up to 5 days. Fold the circle in half, place it in a 9-inch pie plate so that the edges of the circle drop over the rim, and unfold the dough to completely cover the pie plate. Using your thumb and index finger, crimp the edges of the pie shell. Brush the edges of the pie shell with heavy cream to create a perfect, golden brown finish. Set the pie shell to the side while you make the filling.

To prepare the filling, in a medium bowl, combine the pineapple and pomegranate. Set the fruit aside. In a small bowl, whisk together the sugar and cinnamon. Sprinkle the sugar mixture over the pineapple and pomegranate and toss to evenly coat. Place the pineapple-pomegranate fruit filling in the piecrust. Dot the fruit with the butter. Sprinkle the crumb topping over the fruit filling, covering it completely.

To bake, place the pie plate on a baking sheet on the middle rack of the oven and bake it for 15 minutes. Reduce the heat to 350°F and continue baking for 35 to 40 minutes more, or until the crust is golden brown and the juices are bubbling. Transfer the pie plate to a wire cooling rack and allow the pie to cool and set for 1½ hours before serving.

Pineapple-Pomegranate Pie is best served at room temperature or warmed at 350°F for about 10 minutes. It can be stored in the refrigerator for up to 3 days.

Black Plum Pie

Put a fruit bowl in front of me and the first thing I'll go for is a ripe, juicy black plum. The sweet and tart combination of the plums pairs delightfully with the flaky piecrust. If you prefer to go even sweeter, try this quick and easy pie with a favorite crumb topping.

Makes one 9-inch pie, 6 to 8 slices
Level: Easy

Crust

1   recipe Traditional Pastry Piecrust dough for a 9-inch double-crust pie (page 4)

¼   cup heavy cream (to glaze the crimped pie edges and the top of the pie)

Filling

5   cups sliced plums (about 10 to 12 ripe plums, pitted and cut into ½-inch slices)

1   tablespoon fresh lemon juice

3   tablespoons quick-cooking tapioca

¾   teaspoon ground cinnamon

    Pinch of salt

1   cup sugar

1   tablespoon unsalted butter

Preheat the oven to 375°F. Line a baking sheet with parchment paper and set aside.

To prepare the pie shell, on a clean, lightly floured work surface, roll out half the disk of dough with a rolling pin until it forms a 10-inch circle. Set the remaining half of dough aside to use as the pie top after you have completed the filling. Fold the circle in half, place it in a 9-inch pie plate so that the edges of the circle drop over the rim, and unfold the dough to completely cover the pie plate. Set the pie plate aside while you prepare the filling.

To prepare the filling, place the sliced plums in a medium bowl. Sprinkle the lemon juice over the plums and gently toss. Allow the plums to sit for 5 minutes. In a separate small bowl, mix together the tapioca, cinnamon, salt, and sugar. Pour the dry mixture over the plums and mix well. Place the plums in the pie shell. Dot the filling with the butter.

To prepare the top crust, roll out the second half of the dough with a rolling pin until it forms a 10-inch circle. Fold the dough circle in half and place it over the filling, with the straight line of the half circle running down the middle of the pie. Unfold the circle so that the entire pie is covered. Using your thumb and index finger, crimp the edges of the pie together to seal in the filling, and then use a fork to puncture the top of the pie 5 or 6 times to allow ventilation. Brush the top of the pie and the crimped edges with heavy cream to create a perfect, golden brown finish.

To bake, place the pie plate on the lined baking sheet and bake it for 50 to 55 minutes, or until the crust is golden brown and the plum juices are bubbling. Transfer the pie plate to a wire cooling rack and allow the pie to cool and set for 1½ hours before serving.

Black Plum Pie is best served at room temperature or warmed at 350°F for about 10 minutes. It will keep at room temperature overnight and can be stored in the refrigerator for up to 4 days.

Pumpkin Meringue Pie

This pie melds dense pumpkin filling with a light and fluffy meringue topping and the meringue mingles wonderfully with the filling's cinnamon and nutmeg spices. If you have some extra time to spare, I strongly recommend making this pie with fresh pumpkin; it makes all the difference between a tasty dessert and a true culinary experience! For instructions on how to process your own pumpkins, see page 51. (If you aren't a huge fan of meringue, you can make this pumpkin pie without the meringue and still have an amazing, more traditional pumpkin pie. Having said that, I do urge you to try this version at least once.)

Makes one 9-inch pie, 6 to 8 slices

Level: Moderate (Difficult—but worth it!—if you choose to puree your own pumpkin)

Crust

1   recipe Traditional Pastry Piecrust dough for a 9-inch single-crust pie (page 4)
¼   cup heavy cream (to glaze the crimped pie edges)

Filling

1   cup canned or fresh pumpkin puree (if you want to try this with fresh pumpkin, see the instructions on page 51)
2   eggs, beaten
½   cup firmly packed dark brown sugar
1   teaspoon ground cinnamon
½   teaspoon salt
¼   teaspoon ground nutmeg
1½ cups heavy cream
1   recipe Classic Meringue (page 227)

Preheat the oven to 375°F. Line a baking sheet with parchment paper and set aside.

To prepare the pie shell, on a clean, lightly floured work surface, roll out half the disk of dough with a rolling pin until it forms a 10-inch circle. Wrap the remaining half of the dough tightly in plastic wrap and reserve it in the refrigerator for future use for up to 5 days. Fold the circle in half, place it in a 9-inch pie plate so that the edges of the circle drop over the rim, and unfold the dough to completely cover the pie plate. Using your thumb and index finger, crimp the edges of the pie shell. Brush the edges of the pie shell with heavy cream to create a perfect, golden brown finish. Set the pie shell to the side while you make the filling.

To prepare the pumpkin filling, using an electric mixer set on medium speed, combine the pumpkin puree and eggs. Add the brown sugar, cinnamon, salt, and nutmeg. Mix the ingredients together, scraping the bowl several times. Add the heavy cream and mix once again, until all of the ingredients are thoroughly combined. Pour the pumpkin mixture into the unbaked pie shell.

To bake, place the pie plate on the lined baking sheet on the middle rack of the oven and bake it for 40 to 45 minutes, or until the filling is firm in the middle but still soft to the touch. Transfer the pie plate to a wire cooling rack and allow the pie to cool for at least 2 hours.

When the pie has finished cooling, preheat the oven to 400°F. Place the meringue on top of the pumpkin pie, forming a mound of meringue in the middle of the pie. Use a spatula to pat and lift the meringue across the top of the pie, forming peaks. Take care to spread the meringue all the way out to the edges of the crust.

To brown the meringue, place the pie on the middle rack of the oven and bake for 4 to 6 minutes, or until the desired brownness has been achieved. If you have a kitchen torch, you can also use this method as an alternative, but be careful to spread the flame evenly across the entire surface to achieve a uniform look.

Pumpkin Meringue Pie is best served the same day and can be stored in the refrigerator for up to 2 days.

How to Process Fresh Pumpkins

Here's what you'll need:

1 5-pound sugar pumpkin, washed and dried
  Sharp knife
  Spoon
  Steamer
  Cheesecloth
  Food processor

Begin by cutting the sugar pumpkin in quarters with a sharp knife. Use a spoon to scoop out the seeds and clear the stringy matter out of the pumpkin interior.

Place the pumpkin quarters in a steamer and steam for about 20 minutes, or until they become soft enough for a knife to be easily inserted through the flesh. Remove the pumpkin quarters from the steamer and allow them to cool for a few minutes.

Once the pumpkin has cooled, peel off the skin with a knife and place the pumpkin flesh between layers of cheesecloth, then fold the cheesecloth in half. Press down on the pumpkin until the majority of the water has been drained through the cheesecloth. Be diligent: Pumpkins retain a lot of water, so you'll have to squeeze the pumpkin several times.

Place the pumpkin flesh in a food processor and puree until it achieves a smooth consistency. Pour the pumpkin puree into a bowl and voilà! You have an amazing pumpkin puree in a rich shade of orange.

Pumpkin puree stored in a freezer bag keeps for up to 8 months frozen, so be sure to store up during the autumn harvest!

Sugar-Free Pumpkin Pie

This version of traditional pumpkin pie cuts out all of the sugars and uses Splenda instead so that all of your holiday guests can indulge in those comforting and satisfying flavors. As always, you can use either canned pumpkin or fresh pumpkin puree, the latter of which will throw this pie over the edge from spectacular to unforgettable. (For instructions on how to puree your own pumpkin, see page 51.)

Makes one 9-inch pie, 6 to 8 slices
Level: Moderate

Crust

1 recipe Traditional Pastry Piecrust dough for a 9-inch single-crust pie (page 4)

¼ cup heavy cream (to glaze the crimped pie edges)

Filling

2 cups canned or fresh pumpkin puree (if you want to try this with fresh pumpkin, see the instructions on page 51)

½ cup Splenda

½ teaspoon salt

1 teaspoon ground cinnamon

¼ teaspoon ground nutmeg

2 eggs

1 12-ounce can evaporated milk

Preheat the oven to 400°F. Line a baking sheet with parchment paper and set aside.

To prepare the pie shell, on a clean, lightly floured work surface, roll out half the disk of dough with a rolling pin until it forms a 10-inch circle. Wrap the remaining half of the dough tightly in plastic wrap and reserve it in the refrigerator for future use for up to 5 days. Fold the circle in half, place it in a 9-inch pie plate so that the edges of the circle drop over the rim, and unfold the dough to completely cover the pie plate. Using your thumb and index finger, crimp the edges of the pie shell. Brush the edges of the pie shell with heavy cream to create a perfect, golden brown finish. Set the pie shell to the side while you make the filling.

To prepare the filling, using an electric mixer set on medium speed, combine the pumpkin, Splenda, salt, cinnamon, and nutmeg. Then add the eggs and evaporated milk and continue to mix until well combined. Be sure to scrape the sides of the bowl at least twice while mixing to ensure that all ingredients are incorporated. Pour the pumpkin filling into the unbaked piecrust.

To bake, place the pie plate on the lined baking sheet and bake it for 15 minutes. Reduce the heat to 350°F and continue baking for 35 to 40 minutes more, or until the pie is firm in the middle but still soft to the touch. Transfer the pie plate to a wire cooling rack and allow the pie to cool. Once cooled, place the pie in the refrigerator until you are ready to serve.

Sugar-Free Pumpkin Pie can be stored in the refrigerator for at least 3 days when wrapped tightly in plastic wrap.

cream pies

Cream pies can be pretty much anything you want them to be: fruity, chocolaty, or even tropical.

Many people assume that cream pies are difficult to make—probably because their composition doesn't appear to be as straightforward as that of fruit pies. However, this is not the case at all. Cream pies are simply comprised of a base—usually chocolate, vanilla, or cream cheese—and additional flavors and textures are then infused into this foundation to create unique and spectacular tastes.

Although cream pies are relatively simple to make, their tastes are full, rich, and extravagant. What could be more decadent than White Chocolate Raspberry Swirl Pie (page 81) or Oreo Cream Pie (page 73)? Or maybe you want to try something off the beaten track, like Dreamy Nutella Banana Pie (page 69) or Butterscotch Cream Pie (page 61). There are also several National Pie Championship award winners in this chapter for you to sample, including Banana Coconut Pecan Delight (page 56), Orange Creamsicle Pie (page 71), and Peanut Butter Banana Fluff Pie (page 76).

On a more technical note, another great thing about cream pies is that many of them don't require as much baking as other pie varieties (though the crust will need to be baked and the cream will need to be heated over a stove). This makes these pies great for the summertime, when the last thing you want to do is crank up the oven in the heat of the afternoon. Just be sure to prebake the pie shell in the cooler, earlier hours of the day.

Banana Coconut Pecan Delight

In my previous book, I shared a version of this recipe called Mom's Banana Coconut Delight Pie. As I said then, I love sinking my teeth into this dessert because it brings back such happy childhood memories of time spent with my mom. While the original version of this pie is scrumptious, unfortunately it's also somewhat difficult to make. I wanted to find a way to enjoy this comforting taste without the intensive labor. This modified, less complicated version utilizes a vanilla cream rather than a cream cheese base, so the flavors here are lighter and less complex, reminiscent of a tasty tropical drink.

Makes one deep-dish 10-inch pie, 6 to 8 slices
Level: Moderate

Crust

1   prebaked 10-inch deep dish Traditional Pastry Piecrust shell (page 4)

Vanilla Cream Filling

½   cup sugar
¼   teaspoon salt
⅓   cup unbleached all-purpose flour
1⅓   cups whole milk
¾   cup water
3   egg yolks, beaten
½   vanilla bean, halved lengthwise, seeds scraped out with the point of a sharp knife and reserved (or, alternatively, ¼ teaspoon pure vanilla extract)

1   ripe banana, thinly sliced

Coconut Cream Filling

½ cup sugar

¼ teaspoon salt

⅓ cup unbleached all-purpose flour

1⅓ cups whole milk

¾ cup water

¼ cup cream of coconut (I like Coco López, found in the mixed drinks section of most grocery stores)

3 egg yolks, beaten

½ vanilla bean, halved lengthwise, seeds scraped out with the point of a sharp knife and reserved (or, alternatively, 1 teaspoon pure vanilla extract)

⅛ teaspoon coconut extract

½ cup sweetened shredded coconut

1 cup pecans, chopped into small pieces

2 cups Whipped Cream (page 228)

To prepare the vanilla cream filling, in a medium saucepan off of the heat, whisk together the sugar, salt, and flour. Add the milk and water to the whisked dry ingredients and heat the mixture over medium heat, constantly whisking and scraping the sides of the pan. Monitor the mixture carefully; when it begins to simmer and becomes thick and bubbly, after about 4 minutes, let it cook for 1 more minute. You'll know it's finished when the cream thickens to the point where it coats the back of a spoon. Add 2 tablespoons of the heated mixture to the egg yolks and mix them together well. Whisk the egg yolks into the cream in the saucepan and let the cream simmer for 2 minutes, stirring and scraping the sides constantly to prevent burning. Add the vanilla seeds (discard the pod) or vanilla extract and whisk into the cream.

Distribute the bananas evenly across the bottom of the pie shell. Pour the vanilla filling over the sliced bananas. Allow the pie to cool in the refrigerator for at least 30 minutes before preparing the coconut cream filling.

To prepare the coconut cream filling, in a medium saucepan off of the heat, whisk together the sugar, salt, and flour. Whisk in the milk, water, and cream of coconut. Once the ingredients are thoroughly combined, place the saucepan over medium heat. Continue mixing and scraping the sides of the pan as the mixture heats. Once it begins to simmer and the cream thickens to the point where when a spoon is inserted into the mixture, the cream coats the spoon when removed, stir 2 tablespoons of the heated mixture into the egg yolks. Then whisk the egg yolks into the cream mixture, and let it simmer for 2 minutes, stirring constantly. Stir in the vanilla seeds (discard the pod) or vanilla extract and the coconut extract. Add the coconut, mixing until it is evenly incorporated. Pour the coconut cream filling into the pie shell, over the banana cream. Refrigerate the pie for at least 2 hours.

While the pie is chilling, preheat the oven to 350°F. Place the pecans on a baking sheet and bake them for about 5 minutes, or until they are lightly toasted. Remove the pecans from the oven and set them aside until you are ready to garnish the pie.

Once the pie has cooled, fold the toasted pecans into 1 cup of the whipped cream. Using an offset spatula, evenly spread the pecan whipped cream across the top of the pie. To serve, garnish the top of the pie with the remaining 1 cup of whipped cream.

Banana Coconut Pecan Delight should be served cold. It can be stored in the refrigerator for up to 2 days.

Blueberry Cream Pie

My dear friend Gina is the inspiration behind this recipe. Her family's go-to dessert is a blueberry cream pie so, with them in mind, I began experimenting with my own version. This vanilla cream filling topped with fresh homemade blueberry sauce is a straightforward but delectable treat. Be sure to use the freshest blueberries possible for a truly exceptional pie.

Makes one 9-inch pie, 6 to 8 slices
Level: Moderate

Crust

1   prebaked 9-inch Traditional Pastry Piecrust shell (page 4)

Vanilla Cream Filling

½   cup sugar

¼   teaspoon salt

⅓   cup unbleached all-purpose flour

1⅓ cups whole milk

¾   cup water

3   egg yolks, beaten

1   vanilla bean, halved lengthwise, seeds scraped out with the tip of a sharp knife and reserved (or, alternatively, 2 teaspoons pure vanilla extract)

Blueberry Sauce

5   cups fresh blueberries, rinsed and dried

⅔   cup sugar

2   tablespoons cornstarch

To prepare the vanilla cream filling, in a medium saucepan off of the heat, whisk together the sugar, salt, and flour. Add the milk and water to the whisked dry ingredients and heat the mixture over medium heat, constantly whisking and scraping the sides of the pan. Monitor the mixture carefully; when it begins to simmer and becomes thick and bubbly after about 4 minutes, let it cook for 1 minute more. You'll know it's finished when the cream thickens to the point where it coats the back of a spoon. Add 2 tablespoons of the heated mixture to the egg yolks and mix them together well. Whisk the egg yolks into the cream in the saucepan and let the cream simmer for 2 minutes, stirring and scraping the sides constantly to prevent burning. Add the vanilla seeds (discard the pod) or vanilla extract and whisk to combine. Pour the vanilla cream into the prebaked piecrust and allow it to cool in the refrigerator for at least 2 hours.

To prepare the blueberry sauce, in a medium saucepan over high heat, boil 2 cups of the blueberries for 4 minutes. Remove the saucepan from the heat and discard the blueberry pulp by pushing the cooked blueberries through a small-hole strainer. Discard the solids and pour the remaining blueberry juice into a heat-resistant measuring cup to ensure you have 1 cup of juice. If you have less than 1 cup of blueberry juice, add water to the juice until you have 1 cup.

Pour the blueberry juice back into the saucepan and cook over high heat. Add the sugar and cornstarch. Boil the juice for 4 minutes, remove it from the heat, and let it cool for at least 15 minutes. Once cooled, stir the remaining 3 cups of blueberries into the sauce.

Once both the blueberry sauce and the vanilla cream in the pie shell have cooled, spoon the blueberry sauce over the vanilla cream and place the pie in the refrigerator until you are ready to serve.

Blueberry Cream Pie should be served cold. It can be stored in the refrigerator for up to 2 days.

Butterscotch Cream Pie

Chocolate and vanilla lovers are always well taken care of in the dessert arena. But what about those butterscotch aficionados who are overlooked all too often? Well, this recipe is for you! This delectable pie consists of a creamy butterscotch filling layered over butterscotch morsels and topped off with homemade whipped cream. Prepare ahead: Butterscotch Cream Pie should be made at least five hours prior to serving since it will need time to set.

Makes one 9-inch pie, 6 to 8 slices
Level: Moderate

Crust

1   prebaked 9-inch Traditional Pastry Piecrust shell (page 4)

Filling

⅓   cup plus 1 tablespoon unbleached all-purpose flour

1   cup firmly packed dark brown sugar

¼   teaspoon salt

2   cups whole milk

½   cup heavy cream

3   egg yolks, beaten

1   vanilla bean, halved lengthwise, seeds scraped out with the point of a sharp knife and reserved (or, alternatively, 2 teaspoons pure vanilla extract)

2½ tablespoons unsalted butter

½   cup butterscotch chips

Garnish

2   cups Whipped Cream (page 228)

¼   cup butterscotch chips

To prepare the filling, in a medium saucepan off of the heat, whisk together all of the flour, the brown sugar, and the salt. Whisk in the milk and heavy cream. Place the saucepan over medium heat and cook, whisking constantly, for 4 to 5 minutes, or until the cream thickens. Once the cream has thickened enough to coat the back of a spoon, remove ¼ cup of the cream mixture and whisk it into the egg yolks. Pour the egg yolk mixture back in the saucepan and reduce the heat to low. If you are using vanilla seeds, add the seeds (discard the pod) and the butter and continue to whisk for another 2 minutes over low heat. Remove the saucepan from the stovetop. If you are using vanilla extract, whisk it in once the saucepan has been removed from the heat.

Sprinkle the butterscotch chips evenly across the bottom of the pie shell. Pour the cream over the chips. Place the pie in the refrigerator and allow it to cool for at least 5 hours and for as long as overnight. When ready to serve, remove the pie from the refrigerator and evenly distribute the whipped cream across the top. If you choose, use a pastry bag to pipe the whipped cream or an offset spatula to create a more finished look. Sprinkle the butterscotch chips on top of the whipped cream.

Butterscotch Cream Pie can be stored in the refrigerator for up to 2 days.

Chocolate Silk Pie

Chocolate Silk Pie was developed based on my desire to up the ante and create the chocolate pie to beat all chocolate pies. This rich and oh-so-easy pie is encased in an Oreo crust to maximize its chocolate quotient, but you can also use a prebaked Traditional Pastry Piecrust crust (page 4) if you prefer to be a little more sparing with chocolate. Be sure to use pasteurized eggs since this pie is not baked. Finally, please note that Chocolate Silk Pie needs at least three hours to chill prior to serving, so plan accordingly.

Makes one 9-inch pie, 6 to 8 slices
Level: Easy

Crust
1 9-inch Oreo Cookie Crust (page 10)

Filling
3 ounces unsweetened chocolate
12 tablespoons (1½ sticks) salted butter, softened
2¼ cups sugar
1 vanilla bean, halved lengthwise, seeds scraped out with the point of a sharp knife and reserved (or, alternatively, 2 teaspoons pure vanilla extract)
2 pasteurized eggs (see Why Should I Use Pasteurized Eggs?, page 64)

Garnish
2 cups Whipped Cream (page 228)
⅛ cup chocolate shavings
⅛ cup cocoa powder

Why Should I Use Pasteurized Eggs?

Whenever you are making an uncooked pie (or anything else, for that matter) that utilizes raw eggs, it's extremely important that they be pasteurized. Through the application of controlled heat, the pasteurization process gets rid of any harmful microorganisms (specifically salmonella, in the case of eggs) that may be present. Not all eggs are pasteurized, so be sure to check the egg carton before purchasing.

To prepare the chocolate filling, in a double boiler over medium-high heat, melt the unsweetened chocolate until it is smooth. Allow the chocolate to cool.

Using an electric mixer set on medium speed, use a paddle attachment to cream the butter for about 3 minutes, or until it becomes light and fluffy. Gradually add the sugar, mixing between each addition. Cream the butter and sugar together for about 4 minutes, or until you achieve a light color. Add the cooled chocolate. Add the vanilla seeds (discard the pod) or vanilla extract and continue mixing until all of the ingredients are well combined. Add the eggs, 1 at a time, mixing for about 1 minute in between each egg. Be sure to scrape the sides of the bowl on occasion to ensure that all ingredients are incorporated. Once both eggs have been added and beaten for at least 1 minute each, scoop the chocolate mixture into the Oreo crust.

Place the pie in the refrigerator for at least 3 hours before serving. When ready to serve, remove the pie from the refrigerator and evenly distribute the whipped cream across the top. If you choose, use a pastry bag to pipe the whipped cream or an offset spatula to create a more finished look. Sprinkle the chocolate shavings and dust the cocoa powder on top of the whipped cream.

Chocolate Silk Pie can be stored in the refrigerator for up to 2 days.

Graham Cracker Cream Fluff Pie

S'mores, anyone? This pie incorporates layers of chocolate, marshmallow, and graham cracker, all encased in a sweet graham cracker shell. Though most of us associate s'mores with summer nights around the campfire, I like to serve this pie in the winter. Its warm gooeyness is the perfect antidote to a dark, wintery night and provides a nice taste of the summertime to help get you through the more frigid months.

Makes one 9-inch pie, 6 to 8 slices
Level: Moderate

Crust
1   prebaked 9-inch Graham Cracker Crust (page 8)

Vanilla Cream Filling
½   cup sugar
¼   teaspoon salt
⅓   cup unbleached all-purpose flour
1⅓ cups whole milk
¾   cup water
3   egg yolks, beaten
1   vanilla bean, halved lengthwise, seeds scraped out with the point of a sharp knife and reserved (or, alternatively, 2 teaspoons pure vanilla extract)

Chocolate Graham Cracker Filling
1   cup Hot Fudge Sauce (page 223)
5   graham cracker squares, crumbled
½   cup semisweet chocolate chips
½   cup mini marshmallows

2   cups Marshmallow Fluff Cream (page 229)

5   graham cracker squares, crumbled

¼   cup Hot Fudge Sauce

To prepare the vanilla cream filling, in a medium saucepan off of the heat, whisk together the sugar, salt, and flour. Add the milk and water to the whisked dry ingredients and heat the mixture over medium heat, constantly whisking and scraping the sides of the pan. Monitor the mixture carefully; when it begins to simmer and becomes thick and bubbly, after about 4 minutes, let it cook for 1 more minute. You'll know it's finished when the cream thickens to the point where it coats the back of a spoon. Add 2 tablespoons of the heated mixture to the egg yolks and mix them together well. Whisk the egg yolks into the cream in the saucepan and let the cream simmer for 2 minutes, stirring and scraping the sides constantly to prevent burning. Add the vanilla seeds (discard the pod) or vanilla extract and whisk to combine and set aside.

For the chocolate graham cracker filling, pour the hot fudge sauce evenly across the bottom of the graham cracker shell. Sprinkle the crumbled graham cracker squares evenly over the hot fudge layer. Sprinkle the chocolate chips and mini marshmallows over the graham cracker crumble. Cover the chocolate chip and marshmallow layer with the vanilla cream filling. Place the pie in the refrigerator and allow it to cool for at least 2 hours.

When ready to serve, remove the pie from the refrigerator and add the garnish. Evenly distribute the marshmallow fluff cream across the top. If you choose, use a pastry bag to pipe the marshmallow fluff cream or use an offset spatula to create a more finished look. Sprinkle the graham cracker crumbles over the top of the whipped cream. Drizzle the hot fudge sauce over the top of the pie.

Graham Cracker Cream Fluff Pie should be served cold. It can be stored in the refrigerator for up to 3 days.

Maple Custard Pie

This smooth-as-silk custard pie is dripping with a satisfying maple flavor that adds a delectable final note to any meal. There is something very festive about Maple Custard Pie's rich flavor, so it's a great way to top off holiday meals. To really exaggerate the maple flavor, I recommend using Grade B pure Vermont maple syrup; however, if you're unable to procure it, Grade A will suffice. Garnish it with Maple Whipped Cream (page 229) to really take it to the next level.

Makes one 9-inch pie, 6 to 8 slices
Level: Easy

Crust

1   recipe Traditional Pastry Piecrust dough for a 9-inch single-crust pie (page 4)
¼   cup heavy cream (to glaze the crimped pie edges)

Filling

4   eggs
⅔   cup sugar
2½ cups whole milk
¾   cup Grade B pure Vermont maple syrup (you can also use Grade A)
2   tablespoons unbleached all-purpose flour
1   teaspoon pure vanilla extract
1   tablespoon unsalted butter, melted
¼   teaspoon salt

Garnish

1½ cups Maple Whipped Cream (page 229), optional

Preheat the oven to 375°F. Line a baking sheet with parchment paper and set aside.

To prepare the pie shell, on a clean, lightly floured work surface, roll out half the disk of dough with a rolling pin until it forms a 10-inch circle. Wrap the remaining half of the dough tightly in plastic wrap and reserve it in the refrigerator for future use for up to 5 days. Fold the circle in half, place it in a 9-inch pie plate so that the edges of the circle drop over the rim, and unfold the dough to completely cover the pie plate. Using your thumb and index finger, crimp the edges of the pie shell. Brush the edges of the pie shell with heavy cream to create a perfect, golden brown finish. Set the pie shell to the side while you make the filling.

To make the maple custard filling, using an electric mixer set on high speed, beat the eggs. On medium speed, add the sugar and mix. Add the milk, maple syrup, flour, vanilla, melted butter, and salt. Continue mixing until all of the ingredients are evenly combined, scraping the sides of the bowl at least twice. Pour the filling into the pie shell, distributing it evenly.

To bake, place the pie plate on the lined baking sheet and bake it for 45 to 50 minutes, or until the filling is firm in the middle but still soft to the touch. Transfer the pie plate to a wire cooling rack and allow the pie to cool and set for 1 hour before placing the pie in the refrigerator.

When ready to serve, if desired, evenly distribute the Maple Whipped Cream across the top. If you choose, use a pastry bag to pipe the whipped cream or an offset spatula to create a more finished look.

Maple Custard Pie can be stored in the refrigerator for up to 3 days.

Dreamy Nutella Banana Pie

I'm willing to bet that most of us know someone who is nutty for Nutella! Although this rich chocolate-hazelnut spread originated in Italy, over the years it has become an international favorite, available at pretty much any grocery store. When combined with banana and ensconced in a flaky piecrust, this recipe reminds me of a French crepe—simultaneously airy and rich.

Makes one 9-inch pie, 6 to 8 slices
Level: Challenging

Crust

1 prebaked 9-inch Traditional Pastry Piecrust shell (page 4)

Vanilla Cream Filling

½ cup sugar

¼ teaspoon salt

⅓ cup unbleached all-purpose flour

1⅓ cups whole milk

¾ cup water

3 egg yolks, beaten

1 vanilla bean, halved lengthwise, seeds scraped out with the point of a sharp knife and reserved (or, alternatively, 2 teaspoons pure vanilla extract)

3 cups Whipped Cream (page 228), divided into 1-cup portions

½ cup Nutella

1 banana, thinly sliced

½ cup toasted chopped hazelnuts, cooled

Garnish

¼ cup chocolate shavings

To prepare the vanilla cream filling, in a medium saucepan off of the heat, whisk together the sugar, salt, and flour. Add the milk and water to the whisked dry ingredients and heat the mixture over medium heat, constantly whisking and scraping the sides of the pan. Monitor the mixture carefully; when it begins to simmer and becomes thick and bubbly, after about 4 minutes, let it cook for 1 more minute, or until the cream coats the back of a spoon. Add 2 tablespoons of the heated mixture to the egg yolks and mix them together well. Whisk the egg yolks into the cream in the saucepan and let the cream simmer for 2 minutes, stirring and scraping the sides constantly to prevent burning. Add the vanilla seeds (discard the pod) or vanilla extract and whisk to combine. Allow the filling to cool for at least 15 minutes.

To assemble the pie, in a large bowl, combine 1 cup of the whipped cream with the Nutella. Spread the Nutella mixture evenly on the bottom of the pie shell. Distribute the banana slices evenly across the Nutella layer. Pour the cooled vanilla cream on top of the bananas. In a medium bowl, combine the hazelnuts with 1 cup of the whipped cream. Spread the hazelnut whipped cream over the vanilla cream.

To serve, evenly distribute the final cup of whipped cream across the top of the pie. If you choose, use a pastry bag to pipe the whipped cream or an offset spatula to create a more finished look. Sprinkle the chocolate shavings on top of the whipped cream.

Dreamy Nutella Banana Pie should be refrigerated and served cold. It can be stored in the refrigerator for up to 3 days.

Orange Creamsicle Pie

Do you remember the sensation of those quickly melting, sticky orange popsicles dribbling down your chin on hot summer afternoons when you were a kid? I loved that feeling, and I love watching my son, Dakota, have that experience today— cleanup notwithstanding! Happily, this Orange Creamsicle Pie mimics those Popsicle flavors and takes you right back to that childhood feeling . . . minus the dribble. Be sure to prepare for this pie ahead of time: Although it can chill for serving in as little as five hours, it's best if refrigerated overnight.

Makes one 9-inch pie, 6 to 8 slices
Level: Moderate

Crust

1 prebaked 9-inch Traditional Pastry Piecrust shell (page 4)

Filling

3 ounces cream cheese, softened

1½ cups heavy cream

1 14-ounce can sweetened condensed milk

½ cup frozen orange juice concentrate

1½ tablespoons grated orange zest

2 teaspoons orange flavoring

Garnish

2 cups Whipped Cream (page 228)

Grated orange zest

To prepare the cream filling, using an electric mixer with the whisk attachment on high speed, beat the cream cheese until it is very smooth. Add the cream, condensed milk, orange juice concentrate, and orange zest. Mix on medium speed for about 3 minutes, or until the cream holds its own shape and all of the ingredients are thoroughly incorporated. Stir in the orange flavoring. Pour the orange filling into the pie shell, spreading it evenly across the bottom. Refrigerate the pie for at least 5 hours before serving.

When ready to serve, remove the pie from the refrigerator and evenly distribute the whipped cream across the top. If you choose, use a pastry bag to pipe the whipped cream or an offset spatula to create a more finished look. Sprinkle the orange zest on top of the whipped cream.

Orange Creamsicle Pie should be served cold; if you want the real Creamsicle experience, place it in the freezer for a few minutes before serving. It can be stored in the refrigerator for up to 3 days.

Oreo Cream Pie

My son Dakota was so excited when I told him I was working on an Oreo Cream Pie—almost as excited as my husband was. I can't tell you what a huge smile it put on my face when I saw Dakota's eyes light up with excitement as he put the first bite of this pie in his mouth. We had his friends sample our new creation a few days later and they had the same reaction. There's no doubt that kids love Oreo Cream Pie, but be sure to save some for the adults, too!

Makes one 9-inch pie, 6 to 8 slices
Level: Moderate

Crust

1   prebaked 9-inch Oreo Cookie Crust (page 10)

Vanilla Cream Filling

½   cup sugar

¼   teaspoon salt

⅓   cup unbleached all-purpose flour

1⅓ cups whole milk

¾   cup water

3   egg yolks, beaten

1   vanilla bean, halved lengthwise, seeds scraped out with the point of a sharp knife and reserved (or, alternatively, 2 teaspoons pure vanilla extract)

Oreo Filling

1   cup Whipped Cream (page 228)

2   cups coarsly chopped Oreos

½   cup Hot Fudge Sauce (page 223)

Garnish

2 cups Whipped Cream

½ cup coarsly chopped Oreos

¼ cup Hot Fudge Sauce

To prepare the vanilla cream filling, in a medium saucepan off of the heat, whisk together the sugar, salt, and flour. Add the milk and water to the whisked dry ingredients and heat the mixture over medium heat, constantly whisking and scraping the sides of the pan. Monitor the mixture carefully; when it begins to simmer and becomes thick and bubbly after about 4 minutes, let it cook for 1 minute more. You'll know it's finished when the cream thickens to the point where it covers the back of a spoon. Add 2 tablespoons of the heated mixture to the egg yolks and mix them together well. Whisk the egg yolks into the cream in the saucepan and let the cream simmer for 2 minutes, stirring and scraping the sides constantly to prevent burning. Add the vanilla seeds (discard the pod) or vanilla extract and whisk to combine. Pour the vanilla cream into a large bowl, cover it tightly with plastic wrap, and place it in the refrigerator. Allow the vanilla cream to cool for at least 1 hour.

Once the vanilla cream has cooled, fold 1 cup whipped cream into the cooled vanilla cream. Add 2 cups of chopped Oreos, folding them into the cream until well combined.

To prepare the pie, spread ½ cup of the hot fudge sauce across the bottom of the Oreo pie shell. Sprinkle the remaining ½ cup of chopped Oreos evenly across the hot fudge. Spoon the Oreo filling on top of the chopped Oreos. Put the pie in the refrigerator to cool until it is firm, at least 2 hours.

To garnish, spread the 2 cups of whipped cream evenly across the pie. Sprinkle the ½ cup of chopped Oreos over the whipped cream. Using a spoon, drizzle the ¼ cup of hot fudge over the top.

Oreo Cream Pie can be stored in the refrigerator for up to 3 days.

Peanut Butter Banana Fluff Pie

I like to think that if Elvis were to wander into my shop one day, he would approve of this pie. Granted, it *is* lacking the bacon the King required on his infamous peanut butter–banana sandwiches (and the pie, unlike the sandwich, isn't fried). Still, I think it fits the bill.

Makes one 9-inch pie, 6 to 8 slices
Level: Moderate

Crust
1 prebaked 9-inch Traditional Pastry Piecrust shell (page 4)

Vanilla Cream Filling
½ cup sugar
¼ teaspoon salt
⅓ cup unbleached all-purpose flour
1⅓ cups whole milk
¾ cup water
3 egg yolks, beaten
1 vanilla bean, halved lengthwise, seeds scraped out with the point of a sharp knife and reserved (or, alternatively, 2 teaspoons pure vanilla extract)

Peanut Butter Cream Filling
¾ cup heavy cream
4 tablespoons confectioners' sugar
⅓ cup smooth peanut butter

1 cup thinly sliced bananas
½ cup chopped Reese's Peanut Butter Cups

2   cups Marshmallow Fluff Cream (page 229)

To prepare the vanilla cream filling, in a medium saucepan off of the heat, whisk together the sugar, salt, and flour. Add the milk and water to the whisked dry ingredients and heat the mixture over medium heat, constantly whisking and scraping the sides of the pan. Monitor the mixture carefully; when it begins to simmer and becomes thick and bubbly after about 4 minutes, let it cook for 1 minute more. You'll know it's finished when the cream thickens to the point where it covers the back of a spoon. Add 2 tablespoons of the heated mixture to the egg yolks and mix them together well. Whisk the egg yolks into the cream in the saucepan and let the cream simmer for 2 minutes, stirring and scraping the sides constantly to prevent burning. Add the vanilla seeds (discard the pod) or vanilla extract and whisk to combine. Take the vanilla cream off of the heat and set it aside while you prepare the peanut butter cream.

To prepare the peanut butter cream, using an electric mixer set on high speed, mix together the heavy cream and confectioners' sugar until they achieve a thick, whipped cream–like consistency. Fold in the peanut butter until it is evenly incorporated.

To assemble the pie, place the bananas on the bottom of the pie shell. Sprinkle the chopped Reese's Peanut Butter Cups over the bananas. Spread the peanut butter cream evenly over the bananas and Reese's Peanut Butter Cups. Pour the vanilla cream over the peanut butter cream, spreading it evenly across. Allow the pie to cool in the refrigerator for at least 2 hours before evenly distributing the Marshmallow Fluff Cream across the top. If you choose, use a pastry bag to pipe the whipped cream or an offset spatula to create a more finished look.

Peanut Butter Banana Fluff Pie can be stored in the refrigerator for up to 3 days.

Pineapple Coconut Custard with Macadamia Nut Pie

I know that the name of this pie is a mouthful, but don't be fooled! It tastes very light and bright. The pineapple coconut custard will refresh your palate on a warm summer day and the macadamia nuts add just a little bit of crunch to this otherwise creamy pie. Note that this pie should be made at least five hours prior to serving so that it has time to chill. For best results, make it the night before so that the flavors really have time to mingle into one big tropical extravaganza!

Makes one 9-inch pie, 6 to 8 slices
Level: Easy

Crust

1 recipe Traditional Pastry Piecrust dough for a 9-inch single-crust pie (page 4)

¼ cup heavy cream (to glaze the crimped pie edges)

Filling

3 large eggs

1 cup sugar

¼ teaspoon salt

¼ cup unbleached all-purpose flour

1 cup whole milk

1 tablespoon unsalted butter, melted

1 teaspoon pure vanilla extract

3 cups fresh pineapple chunks (about 1 small pineapple, trimmed and cut into ½-inch chunks)

1 cup sweetened shredded coconut

⅓ cup chopped macadamia nuts

Preheat the oven to 350°F. Line a baking sheet with parchment paper and set aside.

To prepare the pie shell, on a clean, lightly floured work surface, roll out half the disk of dough with a rolling pin until it forms a 10-inch circle. Wrap the remaining half of the dough tightly in plastic wrap and reserve it in the refrigerator for future use for up to 5 days. Fold the circle in half, place it in a 9-inch pie plate so that the edges of the circle drop over the rim, and unfold the dough to completely cover the pie plate. Using your thumb and index finger, crimp the edges of the pie shell. Brush the edges of the pie shell with heavy cream to create a perfect, golden brown finish. Set the pie shell to the side while you make the filling.

To prepare the custard filling, using an electric mixer on medium speed, mix together the eggs, sugar, and salt. Add the flour, milk, melted butter, and vanilla and mix until all ingredients are thoroughly incorporated.

To assemble the pie, spread the pineapple chunks evenly across the bottom of the pie shell. Pour the custard filling over the pineapple. Spread the shredded coconut and the macadamia nuts evenly across the top of the custard. Using a dull knife, swirl the coconut and macadamia nuts into the custard until they are incorporated throughout.

To bake, place the pie plate on the lined baking sheet and bake for 50 to 55 minutes, or until the filling is firm in the middle but still soft to the touch. Transfer the pie plate to a wire cooling rack and allow the pie to cool. Once cooled, place the pie in the refrigerator to chill for at least 5 hours before serving.

This pie is best served the next day to allow the flavors to really blend together.

Pineapple Coconut Custard with Macadamia Nut Pie should be served cold. It can be stored in the refrigerator for up to 3 days.

White Chocolate Raspberry Swirl Pie

White chocolate and raspberries are delicious on their own, but put them together and you have a showstopper on your hands. In this decadent pie, fresh raspberry puree is swirled into a smooth, creamy white chocolate filling. The freshness of the raspberries beautifully complements the rich white chocolate. Many people assume that this pie is complicated to make because it looks so elegant, but it's actually quite simple to create this swirled effect. This pie is made with a traditional piecrust, but try it with a Graham Cracker Crust (page 8) to mix things up.

Makes one 9-inch pie, 6 to 8 slices
Level: Moderate

Crust
1 prebaked 9-inch Traditional Pastry Piecrust shell (page 4)

Raspberry Puree
2 cups fresh raspberries
¼ cup sugar
1 tablespoon fresh lemon juice

White Chocolate Cream Filling
¾ cup plus 2 tablespoons sugar
3½ tablespoons cornstarch
⅛ teaspoon salt
4 large egg yolks
2½ cups whole milk
2 tablespoons unsalted butter
3 ounces white chocolate chips
2 teaspoons pure vanilla extract

1 cup Whipped Cream (page 228)
½ cup fresh raspberries
¼ cup white chocolate shavings

To make the raspberry puree, in a medium saucepan off of the heat, combine the raspberries, sugar, and lemon juice. Place the saucepan over medium heat and cook, whisking constantly, for 5 to 7 minutes, or until the puree thickens. Remove the puree from the heat and allow it to cool.

Begin making the white chocolate cream filling while the raspberry puree cools. In a medium saucepan off of the heat, whisk together all of the sugar, the cornstarch, and the salt. Whisk in the egg yolks and milk. Place the saucepan over medium heat and cook, whisking nonstop, for 5 to 7 minutes, or until the mixture starts to bubble and thicken. Once the mixture thickens, keeping the saucepan over the heat, add the butter, 1 tablespoon at a time. Add the white chocolate chips, one third at a time, and continue to whisk until the white chocolate is melted and incorporated into the cream. Add the vanilla. Pour the mixture into the prebaked pie shell and allow it to cool for 10 minutes.

After 10 minutes, spoon the raspberry puree into a piping bag and pipe the puree into circles. You will make a small circle in the center of the pie, then progressively larger ones as you move closer to the edge of the pie. Using a butter knife, begin at the center of the pie and drag the knife outward toward the edge. Repeat this every 1 inch or so as you move around the pie, to create a web effect.

Place the pie in the refrigerator to chill and set for at least 2 hours.

To serve, place dollops of whipped cream around the edges of the pie. Place a raspberry on top of each dollop. Sprinkle white chocolate shavings over the top of the pie.

White Chocolate Raspberry Swirl Pie should be served cold. It can be stored in the refrigerator for up to 3 days.

nut pies

For some reason, it seems that most people consider nut pies to be pretty cut and dry. You've got your pecan pie and maybe a chocolate walnut pie, but most don't seem to explore much beyond those basics. Well, I invite you to start venturing outside of the expected because this chapter is *not* your typical collection of nut pie recipes.

Have you ever noticed that many of the most beloved candy bars contain nuts? I think it's because so many of us enjoy that combination of crunchy, salty, sweet, and smooth. Why should candy bars have all the fun? In this chapter, I've combined these same delicious flavor and texture combinations into pies that will remind you of your favorite candy bar. Almond Joy Pie (page 87), Turtle Pecan Pie (page 99), Candy Bar Pie (page 80) . . . you get it. This is not to mention Peanut Butter Pie (page 93)—with its creamy peanut butter filling and hot fudge to top it off, it's like the world's biggest, most deliciously satisfying Reese's Peanut Butter Cup.

For those times when you're looking to skew toward the more traditional, I've got that covered, too. Maple Pecan Pie (page 91) makes an already-sweet pie even sweeter and the little twist of raisins in Raisin Chocolate Walnut Brownie Pie (page 96) make a surprisingly different and delicious flavor combination.

Almond Joy Pie

Growing up, we didn't have candy that often, but when we did, you could be sure it was an Almond Joy, my mom's favorite candy bar. Today, I still don't have candy bars very often, but I do continue to adore that coconut, chocolate, and almond combination. So, as I am apt to do, I simply transferred all of these flavors into a pie. In this recipe an Oreo cookie crust stands in for the milk chocolate coating of an Almond Joy bar. Coconut flavors are packed into the smooth, creamy pie filling. It took me a while to perfect this recipe, but after many tweaks and adjustments I've created a pie that's just as satisfying as biting into an Almond Joy. In other words, it's a little slice of heaven!

Plan ahead; the pie must be refrigerated for at least six hours before final assembly and serving.

Makes one 9-inch pie, 6 to 8 slices
Level: Moderate

Crust
1   9-inch Oreo Cookie Crust (page 10)

Coconut Cream Filling
½   cup sugar
¼   teaspoon salt
⅓   cup unbleached all-purpose flour
1⅓ cups whole milk
¾   cup water
¼   cup cream of coconut (preferably Coco López brand, often found in the mixed drinks section of most grocery stores)
3   egg yolks, beaten
½   teaspoon pure vanilla extract

½ teaspoon coconut extract

½ cup sweetened shredded coconut

½ cup Chocolate Ganache (page 224)

2 cups Whipped Cream (page 228)

¼ cup Hot Fudge Sauce (page 223)

½ cup toasted sliced almonds

To make the coconut cream filling, in a medium saucepan off of the heat, whisk together the sugar, salt, and flour. Add the milk, water, and cream of coconut and stir to combine. Place the saucepan over medium heat. When the mixture begins to simmer and thicken, after about 3 to 4 minutes, whisk 1 tablespoon of the heated mixture into the egg yolks. Whisk the egg yolks into the cream mixture and let it simmer for 2 minutes, stirring constantly. Then stir in the vanilla and coconut extract. Add the sweetened coconut and mix until it is evenly incorporated into the mixture. Set aside.

To assemble the pie, pour the ganache along the bottom of the Oreo crust. Place the pie shell in the refrigerator for at least 10 minutes to harden the ganache. Remove the shell from the refrigerator and pour the coconut cream into the pie shell. Refrigerate the pie shell again for at least 6 hours and for as long as overnight. Once cooled, remove the pie from the refrigerator and evenly distribute the whipped cream across the top. If you choose, use a pastry bag to pipe the whipped cream or an offset spatula to create a more finished look. Drizzle the hot fudge sauce over the whipped cream and sprinkle the toasted sliced almonds over the fudge.

Almond Joy Pie can be served immediately or stored in the refrigerator for up to 2 days.

Candy Bar Pie

Parents beware: This pie is a sugar high on a pie plate . . . but your kids are guaranteed to love it! Candy Bar Pie is somewhat untraditional for obvious reasons, but the kicker is that it utilizes a pretzel crust. The saltiness of the pretzels is the perfect complement to this otherwise sugary-sweet pie. This is one of those recipes you should feel free to get creative with. I use Reese's Peanut Butter Cups, Twix, and Snickers in this version, but feel more than free to swap them out for your kids' (or your!) favorite chocolate treats.

Makes one 9-inch pie, 8 slices
Level: Moderate

Crust
1 9-inch Pretzel Crust (page 11)

Filling
¾ cup plus 2 tablespoons sugar
3½ tablespoons cornstarch
⅛ teaspoon salt
4 large egg yolks
2½ cups whole milk
2 tablespoons unsalted butter
2 teaspoons pure vanilla extract
3 ounces unsweetened chocolate
4 Reese's Peanut Butter Cups, chopped
1 cup chopped brownie (store-bought will work or see page 170 for my favorite brownie recipe)
½ cup Caramel Sauce (page 222)
3 Twix, chopped into small pieces
1 Snickers bar, chopped into small pieces

2 cups Whipped Cream (page 228)

Assorted candy chunks of your choice, to taste

To prepare the chocolate cream filling, in a large saucepan off of the heat, whisk together all of the sugar, the cornstarch, and the salt. Once thoroughly combined, whisk in the egg yolks and milk. Place the saucepan over medium heat and cook, whisking nonstop, until the mixture starts to bubble and thicken, after 4 to 5 minutes. Add the butter 1 tablespoon at a time. Then stir in the vanilla. Add the chocolate, one third at a time, and whisk until the chocolate is fully melted. Remove the saucepan from the heat and allow the mixture to cool for 20 minutes before continuing. After slightly cooling, add the Reese's Peanut Butter Cups and brownie pieces, stirring until they are thoroughly combined with the chocolate cream.

To assemble the pie, spread the caramel sauce evenly along the bottom of the pretzel crust. Sprinkle the chopped Twix and Snickers bars evenly over the caramel. Pour the chocolate cream over the candy bar chunks. Cover the pie tightly with plastic wrap and place the pie in the refrigerator to chill for at least 2 hours.

When ready to serve, remove the pie from the refrigerator and evenly distribute the whipped cream across the top. If you choose, use a pastry bag to pipe the whipped cream or an offset spatula to create a more finished look. Sprinkle your favorite candies on top of the whipped cream. This pie also tastes great with a little bit of caramel sauce or hot fudge drizzled across the top.

Candy Bar Pie should be served cold, and can be stored in the refrigerator for up to 3 days.

Maple Pecan Pie

In my previous book I shared my recipe for one of my very favorite nut pies, Maple Walnut Pie. Since then, I've played around with the recipe a bit and—I can't believe I'm saying this—I now have a hard time deciding which pie I like better, the original or this revised version, made with pecans. One thing is for sure: Maple Pecan Pie is a great alternative to the traditional pecan pie because it's not too sweet and packs an impressive maple punch. I suggest using Grade B pure Vermont maple syrup to bring out the full maple flavor, but Grade A also works well. To intensify the maple taste, garnish this pie with maple whipped cream.

Makes one 9-inch pie, 6 to 8 slices
Level: Moderate

Crust
1 recipe Traditional Pastry Piecrust dough for a 9-inch single-crust pie (page 4)
¼ cup heavy cream (to glaze the crimped pie edges)

Filling
1½ cups Grade B pure Vermont maple syrup (you can also use Grade A)
3 eggs
¼ cup dark Karo syrup
½ cup firmly packed dark brown sugar
2 tablespoons salted butter, melted
1 teaspoon pure vanilla extract
2 cups pecans, coarsely chopped

Garnish
1 cup Maple Whipped Cream (page 229)

Preheat the oven to 350°F. Line a baking sheet with parchment paper and set aside.

To prepare the pie shell, on a clean, lightly floured work surface, roll out half the disk of dough with a rolling pin until it forms a 10-inch circle. Wrap the remaining half of the dough tightly in plastic wrap and reserve it in the refrigerator for future use for up to 5 days. Fold the circle in half, place it in a 9-inch pie plate so that the edges of the circle drop over the rim, and unfold the dough to completely cover the pie plate. Using your thumb and index finger, crimp the edges of the pie shell. Brush the edges of the pie shell with heavy cream to create a perfect, golden brown finish. Set the pie shell to the side while you make the filling.

To prepare the filling, in a medium saucepan over high heat, boil the maple syrup until it reduces to 1¼ cups. This should take between 5 and 8 minutes, but *do* watch the saucepan to make sure the syrup doesn't boil over; if it does, lower the heat. Once boiled, pour the maple syrup reduction into a heat-proof measuring cup to make sure you now have 1¼ cups of syrup. If necessary, pour the maple syrup back into the saucepan and continue reducing, then measure again. Leave it in the heat-proof measuring cup and allow it to cool.

Using an electric mixer set on high speed, beat the eggs until they are foamy. Set the mixer to medium speed and add the maple syrup, Karo syrup, brown sugar, melted butter, and vanilla. Mix until the ingredients are thoroughly combined, scraping the sides of the bowl at least twice as you go. Once mixed, stir in the pecans. Pour the pecan mixture into the pie shell, distributing it evenly across.

To bake, place the pie plate on the lined baking sheet and bake it for about 50 minutes, or until the center of the pie is firm. Transfer the pie plate to a wire cooling rack and allow the pie to cool and set for 1½ hours before serving.

When ready to serve, remove the pie from the refrigerator and garnish with maple whipped cream. If you choose, use a pastry bag to pipe the whipped cream or an offset spatula to create a more finished look. You may also scoop the maple whipped cream or maple ice cream onto serving dishes to accompany the pie slices.

Maple Pecan Pie is best served at room temperature or warmed at 350°F for about 10 minutes. It will keep in the refrigerator for up to 3 days.

Peanut Butter Pie

It's not often that I find myself at a loss for words, but it's hard to find the right ones to do justice to this peanut butter indulgence. Unlike the Chocolate Peanut Butter Dream Pie in my first book (which incorporates both chocolate and peanut butter flavors), this pie shines the spotlight squarely on the peanut butter, with just a hint of additional chocolate. I know it's hard to believe, but even with all of this richness, Peanut Butter Pie is surprisingly light and creamy. Yet, utterly decadent!

Makes one 9-inch pie, 8 slices
Level: Moderate

Crust
1 prebaked 9-inch Traditional Pastry Piecrust shell (page 4)

Vanilla Cream Filling
½ cup sugar
¼ teaspoon salt
⅓ cup unbleached all-purpose flour
1⅓ cups whole milk
¾ cup water
3 egg yolks, beaten
1 vanilla bean, halved lengthwise, seeds scraped out with the point of a sharp knife and reserved (or, alternatively, 2 teaspoon pure vanilla extract)

Peanut Butter Filling
¾ cup heavy cream
2 tablespoons confectioners' sugar
¾ cup creamy peanut butter

½ cup Hot Fudge Sauce (page 223)

4 Reese's Peanut Butter Cups, chopped

¼ cup creamy peanut butter, softened

Garnish

½ cup Whipped Cream (page 228)

¼ cup Hot Fudge Sauce

2 Reese's Peanut Butter Cups, chopped

To prepare the vanilla cream filling, in a medium saucepan off of the heat, whisk together the sugar, salt, and flour. Add the milk and water to the whisked dry ingredients and heat the mixture over medium heat, constantly whisking and scraping the sides of the pan. Monitor the mixture carefully; when it begins to simmer and becomes thick and bubbly after about 4 minutes, let it cook for 1 minute more. You'll know it's finished when the cream thickens to the point where it coats the back of a spoon. Add 2 tablespoons of the heated mixture to the egg yolks and mix them together well. Whisk the egg yolks back into the cream in the saucepan and let the cream simmer for 2 minutes, stirring and scraping the sides constantly to prevent burning. Add the vanilla seeds (discard the pod) or vanilla extract and whisk to combine. Allow the cream to cool for at least 30 minutes before adding the peanut butter filling.

To prepare the peanut butter filling, using an electric mixer set on high speed, beat the heavy cream and confectioners' sugar until you have achieved a whipped-cream texture. Fold in the ¾ cup

How Do I Soften Peanut Butter?

Simply place the desired amount of peanut butter in a microwave-safe bowl and heat for 20 seconds. Once heated, immediately incorporate the peanut butter into the recipe as directed.

peanut butter until it is well incorporated. Fold the peanut butter filling into the cooled vanilla filling to combine them into peanut butter cream.

To assemble the pie, pour the ½ cup of hot fudge along the bottom of the pie shell. Evenly distribute the chopped Reese's Peanut Butter Cups on top of the hot fudge. Spread the softened peanut butter over the Reese's Peanut Butter Cups. Scoop the peanut butter cream on top of the peanut butter, distributing it evenly. Place the pie in the refrigerator to set for at least 2 hours.

Evenly distribute the whipped cream across the top of the pie. If you choose, use a pastry bag to pipe the whipped cream or an offset spatula to create a more finished look. Drizzle the ¼ cup of hot fudge over the top. Finish the pie by sprinkling the Reese's Peanut Butter Cup pieces across the top. Keep the pie in the refrigerator until you are ready to serve.

Peanut Butter Pie can be stored in the refrigerator for up to 2 days.

Raisin Chocolate Walnut Brownie Pie

I originally created this as a more straightforward chocolate-walnut pie, which went on to become an extremely popular item in my store. Somewhere along the line, though, I discovered that the simple incorporation of raisins really highlights the chocolaty goodness of this pie. The finished product is almost reminiscent of a brownie . . . but with raisins. As if all that weren't enough, it's extremely easy to make. Talk about a win!

Makes one 9-inch pie, 6 to 8 slices
Level: Easy

Crust
1   recipe Traditional Pastry Piecrust dough for a 9-inch single-crust pie (page 4)
¼   cup heavy cream (to glaze the crimped pie edges)

Filling
½   cup chopped unsweetened chocolate
½   pound (2 sticks) salted butter
2   eggs
½   cup unbleached all-purpose flour
½   cup granulated sugar
½   cup firmly packed dark brown sugar
1   cup raisins
1   cup semisweet chocolate chips
½   cup walnuts, coarsely chopped

Preheat the oven to 350°F. Line a baking sheet with parchment paper and set aside.

   To prepare the pie shell, on a clean, lightly floured work surface, roll out half the

disk of dough with a rolling pin until it forms a 10-inch circle. Wrap the remaining half of the dough tightly in plastic wrap and reserve it in the refrigerator for future use for up to 5 days. Fold the circle in half, place it in a 9-inch pie plate so that the edges of the circle drop over the rim, and unfold the dough to completely cover the pie plate. Using your thumb and index finger, crimp the edges of the pie shell. Brush the edges of the pie shell with heavy cream to create a perfect, golden brown finish. Set the pie shell to the side while you make the filling.

To prepare the filling, in a medium saucepan over low heat, melt the unsweetened chocolate with the butter, stirring constantly. Remove the saucepan from the heat and allow the mixture to cool for 10 minutes. Using an electric mixer set on high speed, beat the eggs until they are foamy. On low speed, mix in the flour, granulated sugar, and brown sugar. Add the butter-and-chocolate mixture and mix until all of the ingredients are well combined. Add the raisins, chocolate chips, and walnuts on low speed. Pour the filling into the unbaked pie shell, spreading it evenly across the bottom.

To bake, place the pie plate on the lined baking sheet and bake it for about 45 minutes, or until the middle of the pie is firm to the touch. Transfer the pie plate to a wire cooling rack and allow the pie to cool and set for 1½ hours before serving. Top it off with a scoop of vanilla ice cream for a warm brownie sundae effect.

Raisin Chocolate Walnut Pie is best served at room temperature or warmed at 350°F for about 10 minutes. When covered tightly in plastic wrap, it will keep at room temperature for up to 3 days.

Turtle Pecan Pie

Turtle candies are one of those perennial favorites that defy generational divides. Did you know that DeMet's Original Turtles brand has actually been in production since 1918? It makes sense: It's hard to go wrong with chocolate-dipped pecans ensconced in caramel deliciousness. Well, this pie reminds me of those delectable turtle candies, and it certainly serves up that same sort of gooey, chewy satisfaction.

Makes one 9-inch pie, 6 to 8 slices
Level: Moderate

Crust

1   recipe Traditional Pastry Piecrust dough for a 9-inch single-crust pie (page 4)
¼   cup heavy cream (to glaze the crimped pie edges)

Filling

3   eggs
1   cup sugar
1   cup Karo syrup
2   tablespoons salted butter, melted
1   teaspoon pure vanilla extract
2   cups pecans

½   cup semisweet chocolate chips
½   cup Caramel Sauce (page 222)

Garnish

¼   cup Hot Fudge Sauce (page 223)
¼   cup Caramel Sauce

Preheat the oven to 350°F. Line a baking sheet with parchment paper and set aside.

To prepare the pie shell, on a clean, lightly floured work surface, roll out half the disk of dough with a rolling pin until it forms a 10-inch circle. Wrap the remaining half of the dough tightly in plastic wrap and reserve it in the refrigerator for future use for up to 5 days. Fold the circle in half, place it in a 9-inch pie plate so that the edges of the circle drop over the rim, and unfold the dough to completely cover the pie plate. Using your thumb and index finger, crimp the edges of the pie shell. Brush the edges of the pie shell with heavy cream to create a perfect, golden brown finish. Set the pie shell to the side while you make the filling.

To prepare the filling, using an electric mixer on medium speed, mix the eggs, sugar, Karo syrup, melted butter, and vanilla together until they achieve a cream color. Remove 1 cup of the mixture and set it to the side. Stir the pecans into the remaining mixture until they are combined evenly throughout.

To assemble the pie, sprinkle the chocolate chips across the bottom of the pie shell. Pour the pecan filling over the chocolate chips, spreading it evenly across. Stir the caramel sauce into the cup of reserved filling, making sure to blend them well. Pour the caramel mixture over the pecan filling, spreading it evenly across.

To bake, place the pie plate on the lined baking sheet and bake it for about 50 minutes, or until the middle of the pie is firm to the touch. Transfer the pie plate to a wire cooling rack and allow the pie to cool and set for 1½ hours before serving.

To serve, drizzle the top of the pie with hot fudge sauce and caramel sauce.

Turtle Pecan Pie can be served cold or at room temperature. It will keep in the refrigerator for up to 5 days. When covered tightly with plastic wrap, it can also be frozen for up to 2 weeks.

Pie in a Jar

I love creating mini pies in mason jars for entertaining and gifts. It's such a welcome yet unexpected way of creating a fabulous-looking treat. To make these individual pies, you'll need a wide-mouth, short and squat mason jar (I like to use a ½-pint jar). Use the top of the pie jar to cut out one disk of Traditional Pastry Piecrust dough (page 4) for each jar. Use the remainder of the dough to create a "pie shell" by lining the bottom and sides of the jar. Scoop Mixed Berry Crumb Pie filling (or the pie filling of your choice) into the shell until it's about three-quarters full. Place a dough disk over the filling so that it's flush with the top of the jar. Crimp the edges as you would with a normal pie. For additional decoration, you can use your favorite cookie cutter to cut out festive shapes from the remaining dough and place them on top of the piecrust. (If you'd prefer, you can also sprinkle Cinnamon Sugar Crumb Topping, page 13, over the filling in lieu of the piecrust topping.) If you do not decorate the piecrust, use a fork to puncture the top of the pie 1 or 2 times to allow ventilation.

These jars are designed for canning and preservation purposes, so they are made of thick, sturdy glass that handles heat from the oven well. Simply place the jars on a baking sheet lined with parchment paper in an oven preheated to the temperature indicated on the pie recipe you are using for the filling. Bake the mini pies for 30 to 35 minutes, or until the crust is golden brown. Allow the pie jars to cool before serving. If you are giving them as a gift, tie a festive ribbon around the top of the jar for decoration.

whimsical pies

Like all business owners, I take my product very seriously. But I'm also a firm believer that the actual baking part of my job should be fun. In fact, I think that's a critical element of Michele's Pies' success: When you're having fun, good things happen.

This is why I love whimsical pies so much. For me, a big part of the fun of baking is the creative aspect of it—whether that involves coming up with a unique new recipe or tweaking an old one to test out new flavors and compositions. Getting creative in the kitchen makes indulging in pies more fun, too. Don't get me wrong: I love a traditional pie. But if I were to eat the same pies over and over again, I'm sure they would become less of a treat. It's pies like the ones included in this chapter that ensure your taste buds are constantly on their toes.

I'm all for celebrating as much as possible. So why limit celebrations to the holidays? There's always cause for celebration, even if it's just observing Girl Scout cookie season with my to-die-for Thin Mint Chocolate Cookie Pie (page 116). Also, try familiar flavors in a new format with one of my favorites, Cannoli Party Dip Pie (page 110). Can't decide between cake or pie? Try out Birthday Cake Surprise "Pie" (page 107), a National Pie Championship Winner. Other whimsical award-winners include Chocolate-Strawberry Napoleon Pie (page 112), Lemon-Raspberry Twist Pie (page 121), and Strawberry Napoleon Layer Pie (page 129).

I hope that you'll take a step outside of the common and give these whimsical recipes a whirl.

Banoffee Pie

"What is Banoffee?" you ask. Well, it's my word for a creamy toffee-banana filling encased in a sweet graham cracker shell. This pie is extremely easy to make, though preparing the condensed milk for the filling is rather time-consuming (don't worry— it's just "oven time"). Be sure to prepare this pie at least five hours before serving. If you like, you can top off its whipped cream and chocolate garnish with your favorite nut for an added bit of crunchiness.

Makes one 9-inch pie, 6 to 8 slices
Level: Easy

Crust
1 9-inch Graham Cracker Crust (page 8)

Filling
2 14-ounce cans sweetened condensed milk
3 medium bananas, thinly sliced
   Juice of ½ lemon
1 teaspoon pure vanilla extract

Garnish
2 cups Whipped Cream (page 228)
¼ cup chocolate shavings

Preheat the oven to 300°F.

   Pour the condensed milk into a small, shallow baking dish and cover it tightly with aluminum foil. Place this baking dish in a larger baking dish filled with enough boiling water to reach halfway up the sides of the smaller dish. Place the dishes in the oven and bake for 2 hours or until the condensed milk is a creamy brown caramel color. Remove the baking dish from the oven and allow the condensed milk to cool completely before proceeding.

Place the bananas in a medium bowl. Sprinkle the lemon juice and vanilla over the bananas and toss to coat them evenly. Place the bananas evenly along the bottom of the pie shell. Pour the condensed milk over the bananas and place the pie in the refrigerator to set for at least 2 hours or until the pie is firm.

When ready to serve, remove the pie from the refrigerator and evenly distribute the whipped cream across the top of the pie. If you choose, use a pastry bag to pipe the whipped cream or an offset spatula to create a more finished look. Sprinkle the chocolate shavings on top of the whipped cream.

Banoffee Pie should be served cold. It can be stored in the refrigerator for up to 2 days.

Birthday Cake Surprise "Pie"

Want to have your cake and eat your pie, too? This is the perfect dessert for those of us who can't choose between cake and pie: Now you can have both! Birthday Cake Surprise "Pie" is exactly what it sounds like: an airy vanilla cake wrapped up in a flaky pastry shell. I know it's a little bit hard to imagine, but it is truly delicious. If you want to cut down on prep time, substitute the from-scratch cake recipe below with your favorite box cake mix. You can either bake the cake the same day you prepare the pie, or bake it the day before and wrap it tightly in plastic wrap to store until you are ready to assemble the pie. The sprinkles suggested in this recipe are a super-easy and completely sufficient garnish for this pie's buttercream topping, but feel free to get creative; I also like to use sugar confetti, chocolate chips, butterscotch chips, nuts, and, of course, candles. Be sure to use a deep-dish pie plate to accommodate the multiple layers of cake and vanilla cream.

Makes one deep-dish 10-inch pie, 8 to 10 slices
Level: Challenging

Crust
1 prebaked 10-inch deep-dish Traditional Pastry Piecrust shell (page 4)

White Cake
2½ cups cake flour
1⅔ cups sugar
1 tablespoon baking powder
¾ teaspoon salt
12 tablespoons (1½ sticks) unsalted butter, softened
4 egg whites
1 egg
1 cup whole milk
1 tablespoon pure vanilla extract

whimsical pies

Vanilla Cream Filling

½ cup sugar

¼ teaspoon salt

⅓ cup unbleached all-purpose flour

1⅓ cups whole milk

¾ cup water

3 egg yolks, beaten

1 teaspoon pure vanilla extract

Garnish

3½ cups Buttercream (page 230. Note: If you know you will require more for decorating, double the batch.)

Sprinkles

Preheat the oven to 350°F.

To prepare the white cake, using an electric mixer set on low speed, combine the cake flour, sugar, baking powder, and salt. Add the butter. On medium speed, 1 egg at a time, add first the egg whites and then the whole egg. Slowly add the milk, ¼ cup at a time. Add the vanilla. Beat the mixture on high for 1 minute. Set the prebaked pie shell aside until needed. Grease and flour the 10-inch deep-dish pie dish you used for the prebaked pie shell and pour the cake batter into it. This will ensure the cake fits into the dish properly when assembling the pie.

To bake the cake, place the dish in the oven and bake for 20 to 25 minutes, or until a toothpick inserted in the middle of the cake comes out clean. Place the pie dish on a wire cooling rack and allow the cake to cool completely. Once it has cooled, carefully remove the cake from the dish by running a knife around the edges to easily release it. Once removed, cut the cake horizontally with a serrated bread knife into 2 equal halves so that you now have 2 thin cake layers.

Once the cake has cooled, prepare the vanilla cream filling. In a medium saucepan off of the heat, whisk together the sugar, salt, and flour. Add the milk and water to the whisked dry ingredients and heat the mixture over medium heat, constantly whisking and scraping the sides of the pan. Monitor the mixture carefully; when it begins to simmer and becomes thick and bubbly, after about 4 minutes, let it cook for 1 more minute. You'll know it's finished when the cream thickens to the point where it coats the back of a spoon. Add 2 tablespoons of the heated mixture to the egg yolks and mix them together well. Whisk the egg yolks back into the cream in the saucepan and let the cream simmer for 2 minutes, stirring and scraping the sides constantly to prevent burning. Add the vanilla and whisk until it is evenly combined throughout the cream.

To assemble the pie, place the prebaked pie shell back into the pie dish, pour half of the vanilla cream evenly across the bottom of the pie shell. Place 1 layer of the cake on top of the cream. Pour the remaining vanilla cream evenly across the top of the cake. Add the second cake layer. Refrigerate the pie for at least 2 hours to set.

To serve, spread the buttercream across the top of the pie, decorating as you wish. Scatter the sprinkles across the buttercream.

Birthday Cake Surprise "Pie" should be served cold. It can be stored in the refrigerator for up to 3 days

Cannoli Party Dip Pie

As an Italian, I consider myself to be somewhat of a cannoli connoisseur. In fact, when trying out a new bakery, I generally judge how good the entire bakery is based on their cannoli. So, as you can imagine, I take my own Cannoli Party Dip Pie *very* seriously. Typically each person is served his or her own cannolis, but I like to bring dinner guests together over a shared dessert with this "party dip" version. When served this way, everyone can converse around the dessert, using pastry "chips" to scoop up the cannoli filling. Here's a little tip: Once you run out of pastry chips, be sure to dig into the piecrust!

Makes one deep-dish 10-inch pie and 35 to 40 pastry chips
Level: Moderate

Crust and Pastry Chips

1   prebaked 10-inch deep-dish Traditional Pastry Piecrust shell (page 4)

½   recipe Traditional Pastry Piecrust dough (You will use this ½ recipe to make pastry chips. If you would like more chips, you can always make more pie dough.)

½   cup heavy cream

¼   cup granulated sugar

¼   cup confectioners' sugar

Cannoli Dip

4   pounds ricotta (use cheesecloth to strain the ricotta for at least 2 hours prior to using)

1⅓   cups sugar

1   teaspoon ground cinnamon

¾   cup mini chocolate chips

Preheat the oven to 375°F. Line a baking sheet with parchment paper and set aside.

Lightly sprinkle a rolling surface with flour, making sure that the entire surface is covered. Roll out the half recipe of dough until it is ¼ inch thick. Use a sharp knife to cut the dough into 2 x 2-inch squares. Once you have finished cutting all of the squares, fold each square diagonally, corner-to-corner, and pinch it down the middle. Place the squares on the lined baking sheet and brush them with heavy cream. Sprinkle the tops of the chips with granulated sugar.

Bake the chips for 12 to 15 minutes, or until they are golden brown. Transfer the baking sheet from the oven to a wire cooling rack and allow the chips to cool completely. Once cooled, dust each chip with confectioners' sugar.

To prepare the cannoli dip, using an electric mixer on medium speed, combine the drained ricotta, sugar, and cinnamon. (Add the sugar ⅓ cup at a time, constantly tasting until you achieve your desired sweetness; some people prefer their cannoli less sweet than others, so you may prefer not to use the entire 1⅓ cups.) Turn the mixer down to low speed and add the chocolate chips.

When you are ready to serve, spoon the cannoli filling into the prebaked pie shell. Arrange the pastry chips around the top of the cannoli dip and the platter holding the pie shell and serve the Cannoli Party Dip Pie in a chip-and-dip fashion.

The cannoli dip can be kept in the pie shell for 1 day, but I strongly recommend not putting the party chips into the dip until immediately before serving so that they don't get soggy.

Chocolate-Strawberry Napoleon Pie

Although piecrust is a very traditional pastry, it also lends itself to innovative creations. Here we use thin pie-dough disks to create those layers that napoleons are known for. The trick to this recipe is prep time. Although the individual steps aren't difficult, Chocolate-Strawberry Napoleon Pie includes several layers, each of which requires time to set. Note that this pie requires quite a bit of lead time, since the strawberry glacé needs to chill for six hours before use and the finished pie will need to set overnight. Last but not least, be sure to use a deep-dish pie plate to accommodate all of these wonderful layers.

Makes one deep-dish 10-inch pie, 8 to 10 slices
Level: Challenging

Crust

1   prebaked deep-dish 10-inch Traditional Pastry Piecrust shell (page 4)
½   recipe Traditional Pastry Piecrust dough (to make 2 dough disks)
¼   cup heavy cream (to glaze the dough disks)

Chocolate Ganache Whipped Cream

3   cups heavy cream
1   cup semisweet chocolate chips
¼   cup confectioners' sugar
1   teaspoon pure vanilla extract

Chocolate Pudding Filling

¾   cup plus 2 tablespoons sugar
3½   tablespoons cornstarch
⅛   teaspoon salt
4   large egg yolks
2½   cups whole milk

2 tablespoons unsalted butter

2 teaspoons pure vanilla extract

3 ounces unsweetened chocolate, chopped

Strawberry Glacé Whipped Cream

1 cup Strawberry Glacé (page 225), chilled for at least 6 hours

2 cups Whipped Cream (page 228)

3 cups strawberries: 2 cups thinly sliced and, for garnish, 1 cup whole

Once the strawberry glacé has cooled for at least 6 hours and you are ready to begin prepping the pie, preheat the oven to 375°F. Line a baking sheet with parchment paper and set aside.

Lightly sprinkle a rolling surface with flour, making sure that the entire surface is covered. Roll out the half recipe of dough with a rolling pin until it has a thickness of about ⅛ inch. With a sharp knife, use the bottom of the 9-inch pie dish you are using to trace a circle and create a disk of dough. Repeat once more, making a second disk. Place the 2 disks

Creating Rosettes with a Pastry Bag

Place whipped cream in a pastry bag with a star tip attached. Fold the end of the pastry bag down so that the whipped cream moves to the top of the bag and you can get a nice, firm grip on the end of the bag. Hold the pastry bag perpendicular to the pie top. Squeeze the pastry bag from the bottom, rotate it once, then stop the flow by releasing pressure from the bag. Repeat as desired, either all around the circumference of the pie to create a rosette border or in a few select places around the top of the pie.

perfect pies & more

Deep-Dish Dough

When making deep-dish pies, some people find it easier to use three quarters of the pie dough disk for the piecrust, rather than the usual half. If you choose to use three quarters of the dough for the prebaked pie shell, that is perfectly fine. Simply use the remaining quarter of the dough (rather than half) to make the 2 disks.

on the lined baking sheet. Use a fork to puncture the surface of the disks several times to dock them. Brush the disks with heavy cream and bake them for about 10 minutes, or until golden brown. Transfer the baking sheet to a wire cooling rack and let the disks cool completely. Please note that once the disks are baked, they are extremely delicate. If you want to allow for any mistakes, make an extra disk . . . just in case.

To prepare the chocolate ganache whipped cream, heat 1 cup of the heavy cream in a double boiler over medium heat until it steams. Place the chocolate chips in a medium, heat-proof bowl and pour the heavy cream over them, stirring until smooth. Cool and refrigerate the chocolate ganache for at least 2 hours, until it is firm to the touch. Reserve ¼ cup of the chocolate ganache to garnish the pie; the balance of it will be used to create the chocolate ganache whipped cream.

When the ganache has cooled, continue to prepare the whipped cream. Using an electric mixer set on high speed, combine the remaining 2 cups of heavy cream with the confectioners' sugar and vanilla. Mix for about 1 minute, or until you have achieved a creamy consistency. You'll know it's ready when you can form stiff peaks using a spatula. Fold the finished chocolate ganache into the whipped cream. Set the chocolate ganache whipped cream aside.

To prepare the chocolate pudding filling, in a medium saucepan off of the heat, whisk together the sugar, cornstarch, and salt. Whisk in the egg yolks and milk. Place the saucepan over medium heat and cook the mixture, whisking nonstop, for about 5 minutes, or until it starts to bubble and thicken. Once the mixture thickens, keep the saucepan over the heat and add the butter, 1 tablespoon at a time. Then add the vanilla. Add the chocolate, one third at a time. Set the chocolate pudding filling aside.

To prepare the strawberry glacé whipped cream, fold the strawberry glacé into the whipped cream until they are thoroughly combined.

To assemble the pie, spread half of the chocolate ganache whipped cream evenly across the bottom of the pie shell (reserve the remaining half of the chocolate ganache whipped cream in the refrigerator). Cover this with 1 cup of the sliced strawberries. Spread half of the strawberry glacé whipped cream over the strawberries. Place 1 of the dough disks in the pie shell on top of the strawberry layer. Pour the chocolate pudding filling over the dough disk. Place the remaining cup of sliced strawberries on top of the pudding, spreading them across evenly. Spread the remainder of the strawberry glacé whipped cream over the strawberries. Place the second pie dough disk over the strawberry glacé whipped cream. Refrigerate for at least 12 hours.

When ready to serve, remove the pie from the refrigerator. If you would like to decorate the finished pie with rosettes, fill a pastry bag with a star tip with the chocolate ganache whipped cream and set aside while you evenly distribute the remaining chocolate ganache whipped cream over the top disk. Otherwise, use all of the remaining whipped cream to cover the top disk. If you choose, use a pastry bag to pipe the chocolate ganache whipped cream or an offset spatula to create a more finished look. Using a piping bag with a number 1 tip, drizzle vertical lines of the reserved chocolate ganache across the pie. Then, using the edge of a knife, drag the chocolate ganache down in one direction and up in the opposite direction to create that quintessential chevron napoleon design. If you choose, you may use the chocolate ganache whipped cream in the pastry bag to place rosettes around the edges of the pie (see page 113). Place the whole strawberries across the whipped cream and ganache for decoration.

Chocolate-Strawberry Napoleon Pie should be served cold. It can be stored in the refrigerator for up to 3 days.

Thin Mint Chocolate Cookie Pie

There are few things I look forward to as much as Girl Scout cookie season. I love that little window of time to indulge in those iconic boxes of Samoas, shortbread cookies, Tagalongs, and, most of all, Thin Mints. I know I'm not alone in this! Thin Mints are certainly delicious enough on their own, but my philosophy is to celebrate this all-too-short time of the year by going all out. Make sure you order a few extra boxes of Thin Mints this year; after you've had this pie once, you'll definitely want to have it again . . . and again. Better yet, keep some boxes in your freezer, so you can indulge in this pie throughout the year.

Makes one 9-inch pie, 6 to 8 slices
Level: Moderate

Crust

32 Thin Mint cookies, finely crushed in a food processor
 2 tablespoons whole milk
 2 tablespoons unsalted butter, melted

Filling

 ¾ cup plus 2 tablespoons sugar
3½ tablespoons cornstarch
 ⅛ teaspoon salt
 4 large egg yolks
2½ cups whole milk
 2 tablespoons unsalted butter
 2 teaspoons pure vanilla extract
 3 ounces unsweetened chocolate
23 Thin Mint cookies, processed to coarse crumbs in the food processor
8½ ounces Andes chocolates, coarsely chopped

Garnish

2   cups Whipped Cream (page 228)

10   Thin Mint cookies, crushed coarsely in either a food processor or a plastic bag

Preheat the oven to 350°F.

To prepare the crust, in a large bowl, mix together the Thin Mint cookies, milk, and melted butter. Using your fingertips, combine the ingredients until the entire mixture is moist. Spread the Thin Mint mixture evenly across the bottom and sides of a 9-inch pie plate and gently pat flat so that it covers the entire dish, with no gaps in the crust.

To bake the crust, place it in the oven and bake for 5 minutes. Remove the pie from the oven and allow it to cool completely on a wire cooling rack.

To prepare the filling, in a large saucepan off of the heat, whisk together the sugar, cornstarch, and salt. Once thoroughly combined, whisk in the egg yolks and milk. Place the saucepan over medium heat and cook, whisking nonstop, until the mixture starts to bubble and thicken. Add the butter, 1 tablespoon at a time. Then stir in the vanilla. Add the chocolate, one third at a time. Remove the saucepan from the heat. Add the Thin Mint cookies, stirring until they are combined evenly throughout. Add the Andes mint chocolates and stir until they are melted. Pour the chocolate mint filling into the pie shell, spreading it evenly across the bottom. Wrap the pie tightly with plastic wrap and refrigerate for at least 2 hours before serving.

When ready to serve, remove the pie from the refrigerator and evenly distribute the whipped cream across the top. If you choose, use a pastry bag to pipe the whipped cream or an offset spatula to create a more finished look. If you would like, sprinkle additional crushed Thin Mints on top of the whipped cream.

Thin Mint Chocolate Cookie Pie should be served cold. It can be stored in the refrigerator for up to 3 days.

Key Lime–Blackberry Chiffon Pie

Although this is a somewhat untraditional combination, the lime and blackberry flavors actually complement each other quite nicely, creating one delectably tart treat with the additional twist of meringue folded into the filling. This pie requires a bit of advance planning since the Blackberry Glacé in this recipe will need six hours to cool prior to use and the pie itself will need to cool and set for a minimum of six hours. When serving, I generally cut this pie into smaller-than-normal slices (eight to ten per pie) since the tartness makes a little bit go a long way.

Makes one 9-inch pie, 8 to 10 slices
Level: Moderate

Crust
1   prebaked 9-inch Traditional Pastry Piecrust shell (page 4)

Filling
⅛   cup water, at room temperature
2   tablespoons gelatin granules
2   whole eggs
3   egg yolks
1½ cups sugar
¼   cup cornstarch
    Pinch of salt
¾   cup Key lime juice
1   cup hot water
2   tablespoons unsalted butter
1   tablespoon grated Key lime zest
¼   cup hot water
3   cups Classic Meringue (page 227)
1½ cups Blackberry Glacé (page 225)

Garnish

1 cup Whipped Cream (page 228)
   Grated lime zest
½ cup blackberries

To prepare the filling, in a small bowl, add the ⅛ cup of room-temperature water to the gelatin to soften. While the gelatin is softening (about 5 minutes), in a medium bowl, whisk together the eggs, egg yolks, and sugar. Continue whisking, and add the cornstarch and salt. Whisk in the Key lime juice, 1 cup hot water, butter, and Key lime zest. Transfer the filling to a medium saucepan. Place the saucepan over medium heat and cook, whisking continuously and scraping the sides of the pan frequently to prevent burning, for about 5 minutes, or until the mixture becomes bubbly and thick and almost transparent in color. Add the ¼ cup hot water to the softened gelatin and mix continuously until it dissolves. Add the gelatin to the filling, folding it in until all of the ingredients are combined. Allow the filling to cool for about 30 minutes, or until it reaches room temperature. Once cooled, gently fold the meringue into the Key lime filling so that they are thoroughly incorporated.

To assemble the pie, pour the blackberry glacé evenly across the bottom of the pie shell. Cover this with the Key lime chiffon. Place the pie in the refrigerator to chill for at least 6 hours.

When ready to serve, remove the pie from the refrigerator, and use the whipped cream to decorate the top. I prefer to leave the center of the pie without whipped cream and to place rosettes around the perimeter of the pie to make the colors of this pie pop. Sprinkle the whipped cream with lime zest and place the blackberries on top of the whipped cream.

Key Lime–Blackberry Chiffon Pie should be served cold. It can be stored in the refrigerator for up to 3 days.

Lemon-Raspberry Twist Pie

I work hard on all of my creations, but I worked especially hard on this one, which served as my entry for the Citrus category of the 2011 National Pie Championships. All of my hard work paid off when this pie won first place in both the commercial and professional divisions. Lemon-Raspberry Twist Pie is best made a day in advance as you will want to leave time for the pie to refrigerate and set before serving.

Makes one 9-inch pie, 6 to 8 slices
Level: Moderate

Crust
1   prebaked 9-inch Traditional Pastry Pie crust shell (page 4)

Filling
⅛   cup water, at room temperature
1   teaspoon gelatin granules
1   whole egg
2   egg yolks
½   cup sugar
¼   cup cornstarch
    Pinch of salt
1   cup fresh lemon juice
1¼ cup hot water
2   tablespoons unsalted butter
1   tablespoon grated lemon zest
2   cups Classic Meringue (page 227)
1½ cups Raspberry Glacé (page 225)

Garnish

1 cup Whipped Cream (page 228)

Grated lemon zest

½ cup raspberries

To prepare the filling, in a small bowl, add the ⅛ cup room-temperature water to the gelatin to soften. While the gelatin is softening (about 5 minutes), in a medium bowl, whisk together the egg, egg yolks, and sugar. Continue whisking, and add the cornstarch and salt. Whisk in the lemon juice, 1 cup of the hot water, butter, and lemon zest. Transfer the filling to a medium saucepan and cook over medium heat, scraping the sides of the pan frequently to prevent burning. Whisk continuously for about 5 minutes, or until the mixture becomes bubbly and thick. Add the remaining ¼ cup hot water to the softened gelatin and mix continuously until it has dissolved. Add the gelatin to the filling, folding it in until all of the ingredients are combined. Allow the filling to cool to room temperature, about 30 minutes. Gently fold the meringue into the lemon filling so that they are thoroughly incorporated.

To assemble the pie, pour the raspberry glacé evenly across the bottom of the pie shell. Cover this with the lemon chiffon filling. Place the pie in the refrigerator to chill for at least 6 hours.

When ready to serve, remove the pie from the refrigerator, and evenly distribute the whipped cream across the top of the pie. If you choose, use a pastry bag to pipe the whipped cream or an offset spatula to create a more finished look. Sprinkle the lemon zest and raspberries on top of the whipped cream.

Lemon-Raspberry Twist Pie should be served cold. It can be stored in the refrigerator for up to 3 days.

Lime Pie with Coconut Macadamia Crust

This pie is a delicious study in contrasts, in terms of both flavor and texture. The slightly tart lime filling mingles beautifully with the sweet graham cracker coconut macadamia crust. The light and airy filling and coconut whipped cream topping are wonderfully offset by the slight crunch of the pie shell. It really is perfection in pie form.

Makes one 9-inch pie, 6 to 8 slices
Level: Moderate

Crust
1 prepared Graham Cracker Macadamia Coconut Crust shell (page 9)

Filling
4 egg yolks
3 tablespoons grated lime zest
1 14-ounce can sweetened condensed milk
¾ cup fresh lime juice
¼ teaspoon pure vanilla extract

Garnish
2 cups Coconut Whipped Cream (page 229)
1 tablespoon grated lime zest

Preheat the oven to 350°F. Line a baking sheet with parchment paper and set aside.

To prepare the filling, using an electric mixer set on medium speed, combine the egg yolks and lime zest. Add the condensed milk, lime juice, and vanilla. Continue mixing on medium speed. Be sure to scrape the sides of the bowl to ensure all ingredients are incorporated. Pour the filling into the pie shell.

To bake, place the pie plate on the lined baking sheet and bake it for 25 to 30 minutes, or until the pie is firm in the middle but still soft to the touch. Transfer the pie plate to a wire cooling rack and allow it to cool completely. Once cooled, place the pie in the refrigerator until you are ready to serve. Immediately before serving, remove the pie from the refrigerator and evenly distribute the coconut whipped cream across the top. If you choose, use a pastry bag to pipe the whipped cream or an offset spatula to create a more finished look. Garnish the whipped cream with the lime zest.

Lime Pie with Coconut Macadamia Crust can be stored in the refrigerator for up to 3 days.

Star-Spangled Flag Pie

This themed pie makes a great treat for Memorial Day, Fourth of July, and Labor Day celebrations. Your guests will be totally impressed with your creativity, but the truth of the matter is this pie is extremely easy to make. This recipe uses blueberries and raspberries to mimic the American flag's colors, but you should also feel free to experiment; blackberries and strawberries will also work great with this star-spangled treat. Note that this pie will need to be refrigerated prior to serving and, because of the fresh berries, should be served within 24 hours of completion.

Makes one 9-inch pie, 6 to 8 slices
Level: Easy

Crust

1 prebaked 9-inch Traditional Pastry Piecrust shell (page 4)

Filling

½ cup sugar

¼ teaspoon salt

⅓ cup unbleached all purpose flour

1⅓ cups whole milk

¾ cup water

3 egg yolks, beaten

¼ vanilla bean, halved lengthwise, seeds scraped with the point of a sharp knife and reserved (or, alternatively, ½ teaspoon pure vanilla extract)

Garnish

2 cups Whipped Cream (page 228)

1 cup blueberries

2 cups raspberries

In a medium saucepan off of the heat, whisk together the sugar, salt, and flour. Add the milk and water to the whisked dry ingredients and heat the mixture over medium heat, constantly whisking and scraping the sides of the pan. Monitor the mixture carefully; when it begins to simmer and becomes thick and bubbly, after about 4 minutes, let it cook for 1 minute more. You'll know it's finished when the mixture thickens to the point where it coats the back of a spoon. Add 2 tablespoons of the heated mixture to the egg yolks and mix them together well. Whisk the egg yolks back into the mixture in the saucepan and let the mixture simmer for 2 minutes, stirring and scraping the sides constantly to prevent burning. Add the vanilla seeds (discard the pod) or vanilla extract and whisk to combine.

Pour the vanilla cream evenly across the bottom of the prebaked pie shell. Place the pie in the refrigerator to chill for at least 2 hours, until you are ready to serve.

To serve the pie, spread 1½ cups of the whipped cream evenly over the entire pie. If you choose, use a pastry bag to pipe the whipped cream or an offset spatula to create a more finished look. Using the blueberries for the stars, the whipped cream for the white stripes, and the raspberries for the red stripes, place the blueberries and raspberries strategically across the top of the whipped cream, so that they mimic the American flag design. Place the remaining ½ cup of whipped cream in a pastry bag and pipe rosettes evenly around the edge of the pie (see page 113).

Star-Spangled Flag Pie should be stored in the refrigerator and served cold. It should be served within 24 hours because of the fresh berries.

Strawberry Napoleon Layer Pie

I love this elegant pie so much that my husband, Kelly, and I served it at our wedding. The flavors and structure remind me a lot of napoleons, one of my favorite desserts. I love including strawberries in this layered dessert, but feel free to swap the strawberries out for your own favorite fruit. All fruits meld beautifully with this vanilla cream base. Blueberries or raspberries also work well . . . or try a mixture of all three! Be sure to bake this in a deep dish so that you can really maximize each layer. Also note that this pie should be made about a day in advance of serving since the strawberry glacé will require six hours to cool and set, and the finished pie will require another twelve hours of refrigeration.

Makes one deep-dish 10-inch pie, 8 to 10 slices
Level: Challenging

Crust

- 1 prebaked deep-dish 10-inch Traditional Pastry Piecrust shell (page 4)
- ½ recipe Traditional Pastry Piecrust dough (to make 2 dough disks)
- ¼ cup heavy cream (to glaze the dough disks)

Vanilla Cream Filling

- ½ cup sugar
- ¼ teaspoon salt
- ⅓ cup unbleached all-purpose flour
- 1⅓ cups whole milk
- ¾ cup water
- 3 egg yolks, beaten
- ¼ vanilla bean, halved lengthwise, seeds scraped out with the tip of a sharp knife and reserved (or, alternatively, ½ teaspoon pure vanilla extract)

2 cups hulled and thinly sliced strawberries

1½ cups Strawberry Glacé (page 225), cooled for at least 6 hours

Garnish

2 cups Whipped Cream (page 228)

¼ cup Chocolate Ganache (page 224)

5 strawberries, whole

Once the strawberry glacé has cooled for at least 6 hours and you are ready to begin prepping the pie, preheat the oven to 375°F. Line a baking sheet with parchment paper and set aside.

Lightly sprinkle a rolling surface with flour, making sure that the entire surface is covered. Roll out the half recipe of dough with a rolling pin until it has a thickness of about ⅛ inch. With a sharp knife, use the bottom of a 10-inch pie pan to trace a circle and create a disk of dough. Repeat once more, making a second disk. Place the 2 disks on the lined baking sheet. Use a fork to puncture the surface of the disks several times to dock them. Brush the disks with heavy cream and bake them for 10 minutes, or until golden brown. Transfer the baking sheet to a wire cooling rack and let the disks cool completely. Please note that once the disks are baked, they are extremely delicate. If you want to allow for any mistakes, make an extra disk . . . just in case.

To prepare the vanilla cream filling, in a medium saucepan off of the heat, whisk together the sugar, salt, and flour. Add the milk and water to the whisked dry ingredients and cook over medium heat, constantly whisking and scraping the sides of the pan. Monitor the mixture carefully; when it begins to simmer and becomes thick and bubbly, after about 4 minutes, let it cook for 1 minute more. You'll know it's finished when the cream thickens to the point where it coats the back of a spoon. Add 2 tablespoons of the heated mixture to the egg yolks and mix them together well. Whisk the egg yolks back into the cream in the saucepan and let the cream simmer for 2 minutes, stirring and scraping the sides constantly to prevent burning. Add the vanilla seeds (discard the pod) or vanilla extract and whisk to combine.

To assemble the pie, pour ⅓ cup of the vanilla cream filling across the bottom of the pie shell. Evenly distribute 1 cup of the thinly sliced strawberries on top of the cream. Spread a layer of half of the strawberry glacé across the bottom of 1 of the pie dough disks. Place the dough disk with the glacé facing down on top of the strawberries. Repeat this same layer—the remaining vanilla cream, the remaining cup of strawberries, and the remaining disk of dough, spread with the remaining strawberry glacé and turned facedown—-so that you end with a disk on top. Refrigerate the pie overnight.

To decorate the pie, spread a layer of the whipped cream over the top disk. If you choose, use an offset spatula to create a more finished look. Using a piping bag and a number 1 tip, fill the bag with the chocolate ganache and use that to drizzle parallel vertical lines of chocolate across the pie. Then, using the edge of a knife, drag the ganache down in one direction and up in the opposite direction to create the chevron design typically seen on napoleons. Place the remaining whipped cream in a pastry bag, and pipe rosettes around the edges of the pie (see page 113). Garnish 5 of the rosettes with whole strawberries.

Strawberry Napoleon Layer Pie should be served cold. It can be stored in the refrigerator for up to 2 days.

cookies & bars

In addition to pies, I also like to stock a variety of other sweet little treats in my shops—goodies like cookies, bars, and brownies.

In this chapter you'll find my all-time favorite versions of classic baked goods, such as Fudgy Brownies (page 170), My Favorite Chocolate Chip Cookies (page 141), Peanut Butter Cookies (page 155), Snickerdoodle Cookies (page 162), and Sugar Cookies (page 164). These tried-and-true versions have been refined and honed to the point of perfection over the years.

Also included are a few selections that are a bit more off the beaten track. My family has a tradition of baking as many cookies as humanly possible throughout the month of December. I stash the bounty in my freezer and spread holiday cheer among my friends and loved ones with delicious platters and tins of these cookies made with love. Some of my favorites include Butter Balls (page 139), Oatmeal Lace Cookies (page 148), Chocolate Kiss Cookies (page 146), and Anise Biscotti (page 135).

In addition to cookies, I've also included some of my favorite bar recipes in this chapter, such as Apple Walnut Squares (page 166), Lemon Crunch Bars (page 173), and Raspberry Bars (page 175). As a busy mom, I love sending my son Dakota off to school with bars for class birthday parties or mixing up a batch of these for a quick dessert. Essentially, each of these bar recipes involves a little bit of layering, some oven time, and then you're good to go!

Anise Biscotti

Biscotti are traditional Italian twice-baked cookies that come in a variety of flavors. This particular variety has a hint of licorice flavoring from the anise. In my house, no holiday is complete without Anise Biscotti on the cookie platter. However, they're also a great any-day treat, especially when dipped in a cup of coffee or served alongside a cup of tea. Great taste aside, another reason to love these biscotti is that they will keep in the freezer for up to a month when stored in an airtight container.

Makes approximately 3 dozen biscotti
Level: Challenging

2 cups unbleached all-purpose flour
2 teaspoons baking soda
½ teaspoon salt
3 eggs
1 cup sugar
½ pound (2 sticks) salted butter, melted
1½ tablespoons anise extract
2 teaspoons pure vanilla extract
1 cup chopped walnuts

Preheat the oven to 350°F. Grease and flour a baking sheet or use a nonstick baking pad and set aside.

In a medium bowl, mix together the flour, baking soda, and salt. Set the bowl aside. Using an electric mixer set on medium speed, beat together the eggs, sugar, melted butter, anise, and vanilla. On low speed, pour the flour mixture into the bowl of the mixer and continue mixing until the dough is smooth and firm and all

The Benefit of Nonstick Baking Mats

———

Nonstick baking mats take the place of greasing a baking sheet or using parchment paper. Simply spread the nonstick mat across your baking sheet and place the cookies directly on the mat. These nonstick mats come in various sizes, are easy to clean, and roll up for easy storage.

of the ingredients are well incorporated. Add the walnuts and briefly mix, on low speed, until combined. Remove the dough from the mixer and place it on a flat, floured surface. Knead the dough a little bit to ensure that all of the ingredients are well combined. If the dough is too sticky, knead in more flour, a little bit at a time, until the dough becomes workable. Cut the dough into 2 sections and form each of these sections into a log shape, about 10 inches long and 2 inches wide. Place the dough logs on the prepared baking sheet and flatten them slightly.

To bake, place the baking sheet in the oven and bake the biscotti logs for 25 to 30 minutes, or until the logs are firm in the middle, rotating the baking sheet halfway through the baking time. If you choose, you may bake 2 sheets of biscotti at a time, 1 log on the upper rack and 1 on the lower. When cooking 2 sheets simultaneously, switch racks and rotate the baking sheets halfway through the baking time. Remove the baking sheet from the oven and allow the biscotti logs to cool for 5 minutes. Leave the oven on while the logs are cooling.

Place the biscotti logs on a cutting board and use a serrated knife to cut the logs diagonally into ¾-inch-thick pieces. Place the biscotti cut-side down on an ungreased baking sheet and bake it for 5 minutes, flip each cookie gently with a spatula, and bake for 5 minutes more. Remove the cookies from the baking sheet with a spatula and cool completely on wire racks.

Anise Biscotti can be stored in an airtight container for up to 10 days; in the freezer, they can be stored for up to 1 month.

Chocolate Walnut Biscotti

Chocolate Walnut Biscotti are very popular in my shop, probably because they offer such a lovely medley of flavors: chocolate, walnut, and a hint of orange to finish. If you want to get even more fancy, try dipping the ends of this biscotti into melted white or milk chocolate. For a more everyday treat, serve Chocolate Walnut Biscotti alongside milk or coffee, either of which is great for dipping.

Makes approximately 3 dozen biscotti
Level: Challenging

2 cups unbleached all-purpose flour
½ cup cocoa powder
1 teaspoon baking soda
¾ teaspoon ground cinnamon
1 teaspoon salt
6 tablespoons (¾ stick) unsalted butter, softened
1 cup granulated sugar
1 teaspoon orange extract
1½ teaspoons pure vanilla extract
2 eggs, slightly beaten
1¼ cups mini chocolate chips
1 cup finely chopped walnuts
¼ cup confectioners' sugar

Preheat the oven to 350°F. Grease and flour a baking sheet or use a nonstick baking pad and set aside.

In a medium bowl, whisk together the flour, cocoa powder, baking soda, cinnamon, and salt. Set the bowl aside. Using an electric mixer set on medium speed, cream together the butter and sugar. Add the orange and vanilla extracts. On low speed, pour the flour mixture into the bowl of the mixer. Add the eggs, which will stiffen the dough. Add the mini chocolate chips and walnuts and briefly mix, on low speed, until combined.

Remove the dough from the mixer and place it on a flat, floured surface. Continue to knead the mini chocolate chips and the walnuts into the dough. If the dough is too sticky, knead in more flour, a little bit at a time, until the dough becomes workable. Cut the dough into 2 sections and form each of these sections into a log shape, about 10 inches long and 2 inches wide. Place the dough logs on the prepared baking sheet and flatten them slightly. Using a sifter, sprinkle confectioners' sugar on top of the logs before placing them in the oven.

To bake, place the baking sheet in the oven and bake the biscotti logs for 25 to 30 minutes, or until firm in the middle, rotating the baking sheet halfway through the baking time. If you choose, you may bake 2 sheets of biscotti at a time, 1 log on the upper rack and 1 on the lower. When cooking 2 sheets simultaneously, switch racks and rotate the baking sheets halfway through the baking time. Remove the baking sheet from the oven and allow the biscotti logs to cool for 5 minutes. Leave the oven on while the logs are cooling.

Place the biscotti logs on a cutting board and use a serrated knife to cut the logs diagonally into ¾-inch-thick pieces. Place the biscotti cut-side down on an ungreased baking sheet and bake for 5 minutes, flip each cookie gently with a spatula, and bake for 5 minutes more. Remove the cookies from the baking sheet with a spatula and cool completely on wire racks.

Chocolate Walnut Biscotti can be stored in an airtight container for up to 10 days; in the freezer, they can be stored for up to 1 month.

Butter Balls

My grandma reserved these buttery, melt-in-your-mouth cookies as a treat for holidays and special occasions. I spent a lot of my time longing for Butter Balls, counting down to the next time Grandma would make them. Although the wait used to drive me berserk as a kid, as an adult I'm very grateful for Grandma's holiday-only policy. Thanks to her, every single time I bite into a Butter Ball, I'm flooded with warm childhood memories of happy family holidays.

Makes approximately 3½ dozen cookies
Level: Easy

½ pound (2 sticks) salted butter, softened
½ cup granulated sugar
2 teaspoons pure vanilla extract
1 cup unbleached all-purpose flour
½ cup finely chopped walnuts
½ cup confectioners' sugar

Preheat the oven to 350°F.

Using an electric mixer set on medium speed, mix together the butter, granulated sugar, vanilla, and flour. Add the walnuts and mix on medium speed again. Remove the dough from the mixing bowl and wrap it tightly in plastic wrap before refrigerating for 30 minutes. Once chilled, remove the dough from the refrigerator and use a tablespoon to measure out the dough. Roll each tablespoon of dough into a ball and place the balls of dough 1 inch apart on an ungreased baking sheet.

Place the baking sheet in the oven and bake the cookies for 10 to 12 minutes, or until they are golden brown, rotating the baking sheet halfway through the baking time. If you choose, you may bake 2 sheets of Butter Balls at a time, 1 on the upper rack and 1 on the lower. When cooking 2 sheets simultaneously, switch racks and rotate the baking sheets halfway through the baking time.

Place the confectioners' sugar in a small bowl.

Remove the cookies from the oven and allow them to cool on the sheet for 2 minutes. Then, remove the cookies with a spatula and immediately roll each cookie in the bowl of confectioners' sugar. Place the cookies on a wire cooling rack to cool. Once cooled, sift the remaining confectioners' sugar over the cookies and place them in small baking cups to serve.

Butter Balls can be stored in an airtight container for up to 7 days.

My Favorite Chocolate Chip Cookies

My customers order chocolate chip cookies by the dozens. Hands down, they are the most popular cookie I carry, which isn't surprising because who doesn't love the tasty comfort of the all-time classic cookie? I prefer my chocolate chip cookies big, with a heaping helping of chocolate chips and ever so slightly underbaked to achieve that chewy middle. If you prefer a crisper cookie, add a minute to the recommended baking time. And, of course, if you prefer your chocolate chip cookies with nuts, feel free to add ¾ cup to this recipe.

Makes approximately 5 dozen cookies
Level: Easy

2⅓ cups unbleached all-purpose flour
1 teaspoon baking soda
1½ teaspoons salt
½ pound (2 sticks) unsalted butter, softened
¾ cup granulated sugar
¾ cup firmly packed dark brown sugar
1½ teaspoons pure vanilla extract
2 eggs
2½ cups semisweet chocolate chips

Preheat the oven to 350°F.

In a medium bowl, whisk together the flour, baking soda, and salt. Set the bowl aside.

Using an electric mixer set on high speed, beat together the butter, granulated sugar, brown sugar, and vanilla until you achieve a creamy, light-colored mixture. Add the eggs, 1 at a time, beating in between each egg. Be sure to scrape the sides of the mixing bowl at least twice to ensure that all of the ingredients are incorporated. Once the eggs have been added, gradually add the flour mixture on low speed. Add the chocolate chips and continue beating on low speed until all of the ingredients are combined. Using a tablespoon, measure the dough out into heaping tablespoons. Place the cookie dough at least 3 inches apart on an ungreased baking sheet.

Place the baking sheet in the oven and bake the cookies for 9 to 11 minutes, or until they are golden brown, rotating the baking sheet halfway through the baking time. If you choose, you may bake 2 sheets of cookies at a time, 1 on the upper rack and 1 on the lower. When cooking 2 sheets simultaneously, switch racks and rotate the baking sheets halfway through the baking time. Remove the baking sheet from the oven and allow the cookies to cool on the sheet for 2 minutes before transferring them to a wire cooling rack.

My Favorite Chocolate Chip Cookies can be stored in an airtight container for 3 days.

The Benefit of Cookie Scoops

When measuring out cookie dough, standard silverware teaspoons and tablespoons will certainly get the job done. If you're a frequent baker, though, cookie scoops are definitely worth the affordable investment. Available in all different sizes, cookie scoops, which look like mini ice cream scoops, ensure that your cookies are accurately and uniformly sized and make for a much tidier process by using a built-in mechanism to pick up and release the dough.

Double Chocolate Walnut Cookies

These are one of my go-to cookies to curb those cravings for some gooey chocolate goodness. I prefer these cookies laced with white chocolate chips, but if you like your chocolate straight up, you can substitute the white chocolate in this recipe with semi-sweet chocolate chips. Double Chocolate Walnut Cookies are hard to resist when they're fresh out of the oven, but do your best to save some for those not fortunate enough to be by the oven when done baking!

Makes approximately 3 dozen cookies
Level: Easy

2 cups semisweet chocolate chips
2 cups firmly packed dark brown sugar
½ pound (2 sticks) salted butter
4 eggs
3 cups unbleached all-purpose flour
1 teaspoon baking soda
1½ cups white chocolate chips
1 cup chopped walnuts

Preheat the oven to 350°F. Line a baking sheet with parchment paper and set aside.

In a double boiler over medium-high heat, melt the semisweet chocolate chips, stirring constantly so that they melt evenly. Once they are completely smooth and melted, remove the chocolate from the heat and set it aside while you prepare the batter.

Using an electric mixer set on medium speed, cream the brown sugar and butter. Once creamed, add the eggs, 1 at a time, beating after each addition, until they are well incorporated. Pour the melted chocolate into the bowl of the mixer and mix on medium speed. In a small bowl, combine the flour and baking soda. With the mixer on low speed, slowly add the flour mixture to the bowl of the mixer, a little at a time. Scrape the sides of the bowl while mixing so that all of the ingredients are incorporated. Add the white chocolate chips and walnuts, mixing until they are evenly spread throughout the batter. Measure the dough out in tablespoons and place them 2 inches apart on the lined baking sheet.

Place the baking sheet in the oven and bake the cookies for 10 to 12 minutes, rotating the baking sheet halfway through the baking time. If you choose, you may bake 2 sheets of cookies at a time, 1 on the upper rack and 1 on the lower. When cooking 2 sheets simultaneously, switch racks and rotate the baking sheets halfway through the baking time. Allow the cookies to cool before removing them from the baking sheet and placing them on a wire cooling rack.

Double Chocolate Walnut Cookies can be stored in an airtight container for up to 3 days.

Chocolate Kiss Cookies

As a kid, one of my favorite cookies was peanut butter with a chocolate kiss on top. Even as an adult, I have a hard time walking by these cookies without grabbing one when they're sitting on the cooling rack in my shop, fresh out of the oven with the warm chocolate kiss slowly melting into the sweet peanut butter cookie. Who can resist?

Makes approximately 3 dozen cookies
Level: Easy

1¾ cups unbleached all-purpose flour
1 cup sugar
½ cup firmly packed dark brown sugar
1 teaspoon baking soda
½ teaspoon salt
8 tablespoons (1 stick) salted butter, softened
½ cup smooth peanut butter
2 tablespoons whole milk
1 teaspoon pure vanilla extract
1 egg
Approximately 36 to 40 Hershey's Kisses

Preheat the oven to 350°F. Line a baking sheet with parchment paper and set aside.

Using an electric mixer set on medium speed, combine the flour, ½ cup of the sugar, the brown sugar, baking soda, salt, butter, peanut butter, milk, vanilla, and egg. Continue mixing the ingredients until they are thoroughly incorporated.

Place the remaining ½ cup sugar in a small bowl. Using a teaspoon, scoop the cookie batter 1 teaspoon at a time, roll it into a ball with the palms of your hands, and roll each ball in the sugar, covering it completely. Place the cookies on the lined baking sheet.

Place the baking sheet in the oven and bake the cookies for 10 to 12 minutes, or until they are golden brown, rotating the baking sheet halfway through the baking time. If you choose, you may bake 2 sheets of cookies at a time, 1 on the upper rack and 1 on the lower. When cooking 2 sheets simultaneously, switch racks and rotate the baking sheets halfway through the baking time. Take the cookies out of the oven and immediately place a Hershey's Kiss in the middle of each cookie, being sure to press the Kisses into the cookie completely so they don't fall off when the cookies are cooled. Transfer the cookies to a wire cooling rack and allow them to cool.

Chocolate Kiss Cookies can be kept in an airtight container for up to 4 days.

Oatmeal Lace Cookies

Oatmeal Lace Cookies are so much more than your average oatmeal cookie. These light and delicate temptations (much different from their heavier oatmeal cookie counterparts) are delightfully crunchy cookies that melt in your mouth. One word of warning: Be sure to monitor them carefully during the baking process because each oven behaves differently and these cookies do have a tendency to darken quickly if the oven runs hot.

Makes approximately 2 dozen cookies
Level: Easy

4 tablespoons unbleached all-purpose flour
2 cups quick-cooking rolled oats
2 cups granulated sugar
½ pound (2 sticks) salted butter, melted
½ teaspoon baking powder
1 teaspoon pure vanilla extract
1 teaspoon salt
¼ cup sanding sugar (your choice of color)

Preheat the oven to 375°F.

Using an electric mixer set on medium speed, mix the flour, oats, granulated sugar, melted butter, baking powder, vanilla, and salt until they are thoroughly combined. Scrape the sides of the bowl while mixing to ensure that all of the ingredients are incorporated. Measure the dough out in tablespoons and place the dollops of dough at least 4 inches apart on an ungreased baking sheet.

Place the baking sheet in the oven and bake the cookies for 8 to 10 minutes, or until the edges of the cookies turn golden brown, rotating the baking sheet halfway through the baking time. If you choose, you may bake 2 sheets of cookies at a time, 1 on the upper rack and 1 on the lower. When cooking 2 sheets simultaneously, switch racks and rotate the baking sheets halfway through the baking time. Remember to watch these cookies carefully as they burn easily and cooking time varies from oven to oven. Remove the cookies from the oven and sprinkle them with your favorite sanding sugar. Allow the cookies to cool completely before removing them from the baking sheet with a spatula.

Oatmeal Lace Cookies will keep in an airtight container for at least 1 week. Take care when packing them for storage as these cookies are very thin and break easily.

Oatmeal Cranberry Walnut Cookies

Pretty much every baker has her own version of an oatmeal-raisin cookie. While I love those cookies, I decided that I wanted to add my own little twist to this traditional cookie by substituting dried cranberries for the more traditional raisins.

Makes approximately 2 dozen cookies
Level: Easy

½   pound (2 sticks) salted butter, softened
⅓   cup granulated sugar
1   cup firmly packed dark brown sugar
1   large egg
⅛   cup water
1   teaspoon pure vanilla extract
1   cup unbleached all-purpose flour
2   cups quick-cooking rolled oats
1   teaspoon ground cinnamon
¼   teaspoon baking powder
¼   teaspoon baking soda
½   cup dried cranberries
½   cup chopped walnuts

Preheat the oven to 350°F. Line a baking sheet with parchment paper and set aside.

Using an electric mixer set on medium speed, mix together the butter, granulated sugar, and brown sugar. Scrape the sides of the bowl while mixing to ensure that all of the ingredients are incorporated. Add the egg, water, and vanilla.

In a separate large bowl, whisk together the flour, oats, cinnamon, baking powder, and baking soda. On low speed, gradually add this flour mixture to the butter mixture, again scraping the sides of the bowl. Once combined, add the cranberries and walnuts and stir until they are well combined. Measure the dough out in tablespoons and place the dollops of dough 2 inches apart on the lined baking sheet.

Place the baking sheet in the oven and bake the cookies for 15 to 18 minutes, or until the edges of the cookies are brown, rotating the baking sheet halfway through the baking time. If you choose, you may bake 2 sheets of cookies at a time, 1 on the upper rack and 1 on the lower. When cooking 2 sheets simultaneously, switch racks and rotate the baking sheets halfway through the baking time. Remove the sheet from the oven and allow the cookies to cool for 2 minutes while still on the baking sheet. Transfer them to a wire cooling rack to finish cooling.

Oatmeal Cranberry Walnut Cookies can be stored in an airtight container at room temperature for 3 days.

Pastry Cutout Cookies with Raspberry-Almond Cream Cheese Filling

With their layers of almond cream cheese and raspberry jam and their drizzle of white chocolate, these cookies are the perfect, easy-to-make treat for Valentine's Day. Even better, since these are cutout cookies, I use a heart-shaped cookie cutter for the pastry cookie base, and voilà! Of course, by simply swapping out a heart-shaped cookie cutter for a different design, you can tailor these cookies to whatever holiday (or everyday) occasion you wish. It's also fun to play around with the sandwich filling. If almond and raspberry flavors aren't your style, try substituting your favorite jam along with Chocolate Whipped Cream (page 228), or folding Strawberry Glacé (page 225) into regular Whipped Cream (page 228). Experiment and have fun with this one!

Makes approximately 2 dozen medium-size cookies
Level: Challenging

1 recipe Traditional Pastry Piecrust dough (see page 4)
¼ cup heavy cream
3 tablespoons granulated sugar
6 ounces cream cheese, softened
5 tablespoons salted butter, softened
⅔ cup confectioners' sugar
2 teaspoons almond extract
1 10-ounce jar seedless raspberry jam
1 cup white chocolate chips
  Red sanding sugar (or the color of your choice)

Preheat the oven to 400°F. Line 2 or 3 baking sheets with parchment paper and set aside.

Lightly sprinkle a rolling surface with flour, making sure that the entire surface is covered. Divide the ball of piecrust dough into 4 sections. Take 1 of the sections and roll it out to ¼-inch thickness. Use a 2- to 3-inch cookie cutter to cut out the pastry cookies. Place the cookies on the lined baking sheet, making sure that the cookies are at least 2 inches apart. Set the sheet of finished cookies aside and repeat the above steps with each of the 3 remaining sections of dough. You will want to end with an even number of cookies. Using a pastry brush, brush each cookie with the heavy cream, and sprinkle half of the cookies with the granulated sugar.

Place the cookies in the oven and bake for 7 to 10 minutes, or until the cookies are golden brown, rotating the baking sheet halfway through the baking time. If you choose, you may bake 2 sheets of cookies at a time, 1 on the upper rack and 1 on the lower. When cooking 2 sheets simultaneously, switch racks and rotate the baking sheets halfway through the baking time. Allow the cookies to cool on the baking sheet before removing them. Divide the cookies into 2 batches: those that are covered with granulated sugar and those that are not.

As the cookies are cooling, you may begin to prepare the filling. Using an electric mixer set on medium speed, mix together the cream cheese, 1 tablespoons of the butter, the confectioners' sugar, and the almond extract until they are well combined.

To assemble the cookies, spread a layer of the cream cheese mixture on the bottom side of each cookie not sprinkled with granulated sugar. Use an offset spatula to spread a layer of the raspberry jam over the cream cheese mixture. Make cookie sandwiches by placing the cookies with the granulated sugar on top of the raspberry jam, making sure the side with the granulated sugar is facing up.

Place the white chocolate chips and the remaining 1 tablespoon butter in a small microwavable bowl. Microwave for about 1 minute, or until the chocolate is just melted. Stir gently to combine until smooth. Place the chocolate mixture into a pastry bag or a resealable plastic bag with 1 corner cut out (this should be a small snip). Drizzle the chocolate over the sandwich cookies and sprinkle the chocolate with red sanding sugar as a garnish.

Pastry Cutout Cookies with Raspberry-Almond Cream Cheese Filling should be served immediately or kept in the refrigerator until you are ready to serve. They will keep for up to 2 days.

Peanut Butter Cookies

Who doesn't appreciate the homey richness of a good old-fashioned peanut butter cookie? While they're absolutely a great everyday treat, my family loves them so much that we also always have a fresh batch on the holidays. To dress them up for special occasions, we sprinkle colored sanding sugar over the traditional crosshatching. Whether it's a holiday or just any day, enjoy this cookie with a cup of piping-hot coffee or a mug of hot chocolate.

Makes 3 dozen cookies
Level: Easy

    8 tablespoons (1 stick) salted butter, softened
    ½ cup creamy peanut butter
    ½ cup granulated sugar
    ½ cup firmly packed dark brown sugar
    1 egg
 1¼ cups unbleached all-purpose flour
    ½ teaspoon baking powder
    ¼ teaspoon baking soda
    ¼ teaspoon salt
    ½ cup chopped unsalted peanuts
    ½ cup granulated sugar or colored sanding sugar (your choice of color)

Preheat the oven to 375°F. Line a baking sheet with parchment paper and set aside.

Using an electric mixer set on medium speed, mix together the butter, peanut butter, ½ cup of the granulated sugar, the brown sugar, and the egg. Once the mixture is well combined, add the flour, baking powder, baking soda, and salt. Mix them together on low speed until the flour is incorporated; then turn the mixer up to medium speed until all of the ingredients are well combined. Add the peanuts and, on low speed, briefly mix. Wrap the dough tightly in plastic wrap and put it in the refrigerator to chill for at least 30 minutes.

Once the dough is chilled, measure it into heaping teaspoons, then roll each teaspoon into a ball. Place the remaining ½ cup sugar in a small bowl and roll each ball of dough through the sugar, coating completely. Reserve the remaining sugar. Place the balls 2 inches apart on the prepared baking sheet.

Place the baking sheet in the oven and bake the cookies for 10 to 12 minutes, rotating the baking sheet halfway through the baking time. If you choose, you may bake 2 sheets of cookies at a time, 1 on the upper rack and 1 on the lower. When cooking 2 sheets simultaneously, switch racks and rotate the baking sheets halfway through the baking time. Upon removing the cookies from the oven, use a fork to form a crosshatch indentation on the top of each cookie. Sprinkle the remaining granulated sugar or colored sanding sugar over the top of each cookie. Allow the cookies to cool completely before removing them from the baking sheet.

Peanut Butter Cookies can be stored in an airtight container for up to 7 days.

perfect pies & more

Pecan Crescent Cookies

Rich, buttery, and totally irresistible, these old-fashioned Italian nut cookies were another of my grandmother's specialties. Pecan Crescents are so light and delicate that it's hard not to grab a handful at a time. I like to add mini chocolate chips, but if you prefer the nut flavor straight up, feel free to omit the chocolate chips. As for which way is the "right" way, some Italians will tell you that chocolate chips are traditional and others will wonder why you would ever consider messing with the simplicity of this pecan flavor by adding chocolate chips. I'll leave it to you to decide which way is best.

Makes 4½ dozen cookies
Level: Easy

1 cup pecans, chopped into small pieces
1 cup confectioners' sugar
½ pound (2 sticks) unsalted butter, softened
1½ teaspoons pure vanilla extract
2 cups unbleached all-purpose flour
¼ teaspoon salt
½ cup mini semisweet chocolate chips (optional)

Preheat the oven to 350°F.

In a small bowl, combine the pecans with ¼ cup of the confectioners' sugar. Set the bowl aside. Using an electric mixer set at medium speed, mix together ¼ cup confectioners' sugar, the butter, and the vanilla. Pour the sugar-pecan mixture into the butter mixture and mix on medium speed until all of the ingredients are well combined. In a separate bowl, whisk together the flour and salt. Add the flour mixture to the butter-pecan mixture and mix on medium speed until all of the ingredients are well combined. If you choose to incorporate chocolate chips, mix them in.

Working with 1 tablespoon of dough at a time, form the dough into crescent shapes. Place the crescents 2 inches apart on an ungreased baking sheet.

Place the baking sheet in the oven and bake the cookies for 12 to 14 minutes, or until they are slightly browned, rotating the baking sheet halfway through the baking time. If you choose, you may bake 2 sheets of cookies at a time, 1 on the upper rack and 1 on the lower. When cooking 2 sheets simultaneously, switch racks and rotate the baking sheets halfway through the baking time.

Place the remaining ½ cup confectioners' sugar in a small bowl. When the cookies come out of the oven, immediately roll the crescent cookies in the bowl of confectioners' sugar, then place them on a wire cooling rack to cool. When you are ready to serve the cookies, sift them with the remaining confectioners' sugar.

Pecan Crescent Cookies can be kept in an airtight container for up to 7 days.

Raspberry Linzer Cookies

In case you don't know, a Raspberry Linzer Cookie is composed of two hazelnut cookies sandwiched together with raspberry jam in the middle, in the tradition of the linzer tart. These cookies absolutely melt in your mouth. Although this recipe uses raspberry jam, feel free to experiment with different flavors. I also like to use apricot and strawberry, and sometimes I use a few different jams in a single batch of linzers to provide some options on my cookie platter. If you can't locate hazelnut flour in your local grocery store, most specialty food stores carry it. Both seasonal and everyday linzer cookie cutters can be purchased in sets at most kitchen stores. Linzer sets have two different sized cutters, one larger and one smaller for the cutout. If you are unable to find a linzer set, just use two different-size cookie cutters.

Makes approximately 60 small- or 30 medium-size cookie sandwiches
Level: Moderate

½ pound (2 sticks) salted butter, softened
⅔ cup granulated sugar
1¼ cups confectioners' sugar
1 teaspoon baking powder
1 teaspoon ground cinnamon
2½ teaspoons pure vanilla extract
1 large egg
2¼ cups unbleached all-purpose flour
1 cup hazelnut flour
1 cup seedless raspberry jam (or, alternatively, the fruit jam of your choice)

Using an electric mixer set on medium speed, beat together the butter, granulated sugar, ¾ cup of the confectioners' sugar, the baking powder, the cinnamon, and the vanilla. Be sure to scrape the sides of the bowl to ensure that all of the ingredients are incorporated. Add the egg and continue mixing on medium speed.

In a separate bowl, whisk together the unbleached all-purpose flour and hazelnut flour. Set the mixer to low and add the flour mixture to the batter, mixing until all of the ingredients are well incorporated. Remove the dough from the bowl and divide it in half. Wrap both halves tightly in plastic wrap and place them in the refrigerator. Allow the dough to chill for 30 minutes (this will make rolling the dough easier).

Preheat the oven to 375°F.

Lightly sprinkle a rolling surface with flour, making sure that the entire surface is covered. Take 1 of the halves of dough and roll it out until it is ⅛ inch thick. Use the larger cutter to cut out the cookie bottoms. Once you have finished the first half of dough, roll the second half, again until it is ⅛ inch thick. This time, you will cut the cookie tops; then, use the smaller cutter to cut into the center of the cookie to create the design. By the time you finish cutting, you should have an equal number of cookie bottoms and tops. Transfer the cookies to an ungreased baking sheet.

Place the baking sheet in the oven and bake the cookies for 8 to 10 minutes, or until they are slightly browned around the edges, rotating the baking sheet halfway through the baking time. If you choose, you may cook 2 sheets of cookies at a time, 1 on the upper rack and 1 on the lower. When cooking 2 sheets simultaneously, switch racks and rotate the baking sheets halfway through the baking time. When they are done, remove the cookies from the baking sheet and transfer them to a wire cooling rack.

Once the cookies have thoroughly cooled, spread the raspberry preserves onto the bottom half of the cookie. (Note: Only spread the raspberry preserve on the number of cookies that you will use that day.) Sift the remaining ½ cup of confectioners' sugar over the top of the cookies right before serving. Then place the cookie tops over the bottoms to create a cookie sandwich.

Raspberry Linzer Cookies without the raspberry preserve can be kept in an airtight container for up to 7 days. Make the sandwiches as needed.

Snickerdoodle Cookies

Every baker should have a snickerdoodle recipe in his or her repertoire. These soft and pliable cinnamon-sugar treats are oh-so-easy to make and sinfully delicious.

Makes approximately 2 dozen cookies
Level: Easy

8 tablespoons (1 stick) salted butter, softened
½ cup shortening
1½ cups plus 3 tablespoons sugar
2 large eggs
2 teaspoons pure vanilla extract
2¾ cups unbleached all-purpose flour
2 teaspoons cream of tartar
1 teaspoon baking soda
¼ teaspoon salt
3 tablespoons ground cinnamon

Preheat the oven to 350°F. Line a baking sheet with parchment paper and set aside.

Using an electric mixer set on medium speed, beat the butter and shortening until the mixture is light and creamy. Gradually add the 1½ cups of sugar, ½ cup at a time. Add the eggs, 1 at a time. Once the eggs are mixed in, add the vanilla.

In a separate bowl, whisk together the flour, cream of tartar, baking soda, and salt. Set the mixer to low speed and slowly add the dry ingredients to the batter. Once the ingredients are slightly combined, turn the mixer up to medium speed and continue mixing until all of the ingredients are thoroughly combined. Remove the bowl and cover it with plastic wrap. Place the covered bowl in the refrigerator and allow it to chill for about 20 minutes.

In a small, shallow dish, whisk together the 3 tablespoons of sugar and the cinnamon. Measure the dough out into tablespoons and roll each tablespoon of dough into a ball. Then, roll each ball of dough through the cinnamon-sugar mixture before placing them 2 inches apart on the lined baking sheet.

Place the baking sheet on the middle rack of the oven and bake the cookies for 10 to 12 minutes, or until the edges of the cookies are brown and the middle is pale brown, rotating the baking sheet halfway through the baking time. If you choose, you may bake 2 sheets of cookies at a time, 1 on the upper rack and 1 on the lower. When cooking 2 sheets simultaneously, switch racks and rotate the baking sheets halfway through the baking time. Allow the cookies to cool on the sheet for 2 minutes, then transfer them to a wire cooling rack to finish cooling.

Snickerdoodles can be stored in an airtight container at room temperature for 3 days.

Sugar Cookies

As a kid, I had so much fun making sugar cookies and cutting them into whatever shapes my little heart desired. Today, my son Dakota and I frequently bake sugar cookies together, too. This is a great introductory recipe to get the child in your life interested in the kitchen. Kids love to roll the dough and cut the cookies into their favorite shapes, whether it's butterflies or a football. Dakota and I like to frost our sugar cookies with Royal Icing (page 231), but if you want to save some time, just sprinkle colored sanding sugar over the tops of the cookies before baking.

Makes approximately 2 dozen medium-size cookies
Level: Easy

1	cup sugar
12	tablespoons (1½ sticks) unsalted butter, softened
1	egg
½	teaspoon salt
1	teaspoon grated lemon zest
1½	teaspoons pure vanilla extract
2½	cups unbleached all-purpose flour
1	teaspoon baking powder
1	recipe Royal Icing (page 231) or colored sanding sugar

Preheat the oven to 350°F. Line a baking sheet with parchment paper and set aside.

Using an electric mixer set on medium speed, beat together the sugar and butter. Once you have achieved a cream color, add the egg while continuing to beat on medium speed. Add the salt, lemon zest, vanilla, flour, and baking powder, continuing to mix until all of the ingredients are well combined. Be sure to scrape the sides of the bowl several times to ensure that all of the ingredients are well incorporated.

Lightly sprinkle a rolling surface with flour, making sure that the entire surface is covered. Divide the dough into workable pieces and roll it out over your work surface until it is ¼ inch thick. Then, using the cookie cutter of your choice, cut the dough. (Sprinkle the sanding sugar across the top of the cut cookies at this point if you are decorating the cookies with it.) Place the sugar cookies on the lined baking sheet.

Place the baking sheet in the oven and bake the cookies for 10 to 12 minutes, or until they are slightly brown around the edges, rotating the baking sheet halfway through the baking time. If you choose, you may bake 2 sheets of cookies at a time, 1 on the upper rack and 1 on the lower. When cooking 2 sheets simultaneously, switch racks and rotate the baking sheets halfway through the baking time. Remove the baking sheet from the oven and place the cookies on a wire cooling rack. If you are decorating them with royal icing, allow them to cool completely before frosting. Once you have finished frosting, allow the royal icing to harden completely before serving or storing the cookies.

Sugar Cookies can be stored in an airtight container for up to 4 days.

Apple Walnut Squares

If you like starting your day with a sweet treat, Apple Walnut Squares are the perfect addition to an autumnal breakfast or brunch. With fresh apples and a healthy dose of chopped walnuts, as far as sweets go, this is practically healthy! If you prefer to save your sweets for later in the day, Apple Walnut Squares are also great slightly warmed, with a scoop of vanilla ice cream on top.

Makes approximately 2 dozen 2 x 2-inch squares
Level: Easy

2   cups unbleached all-purpose flour
2   cups firmly packed dark brown sugar
8   tablespoons (1 stick) salted butter, softened
1   cup chopped walnuts
1   teaspoon ground cinnamon
1   teaspoon baking soda
½   teaspoon salt
1   egg
1   cup sour cream
1   teaspoon pure vanilla extract
2   cups chopped apples (about 3 apples, cored, peeled, and chopped)

Preheat the oven to 350°F. Grease a 9 x 13-inch baking dish and set aside.

To prepare the squares, in a medium bowl, use a pastry blender to mix together the flour, brown sugar, and butter until the butter is in pea-size pieces. Stir in the walnuts. Remove 2 cups of the mixture and press it into the bottom of the greased baking dish. Add the cinnamon, baking soda, and salt to the remaining mixture, then place the entire mixture in the bowl of an electric mixer. With the mixer set on low speed, beat in the egg, sour cream, and vanilla. Once combined, gently stir in the apples. Spoon the batter into the prepared baking dish, spreading it evenly across the bottom layer.

Place the pan on the middle rack of the oven and bake it for 35 to 40 minutes, or until a wooden toothpick inserted in the center of the pan comes out clean. Allow it to cool before cutting 2 x 2-inch squares and serving.

Apple Walnut Squares can be kept tightly wrapped in plastic wrap for up to 2 days.

Blondies

Before opening my flagship pie shop, I searched through my mom's recipe box for all of my favorites. At that point, it had been years since I'd tasted a blondie, which is essentially a chocolate chip cookie in bar form. Since reacquainting myself with this recipe, I've started baking it frequently and these treats have become a top seller in my stores. Blondies are the perfect quick fix for occasions when you don't have time to do something complicated, but want to offer something more exciting than a standard cookie. My son Dakota always requests blondies to distribute to his class for birthdays and they're a *huge* hit with the kids!

Makes approximately 2 dozen 2 x 2-inch bars
Level: Easy

  2 cups unbleached all-purpose flour
  2 cups firmly packed dark brown sugar
  ½ pound (2 sticks) salted butter, softened
  1 teaspoon baking powder
  ½ teaspoon salt
  ½ teaspoon baking soda
  2 eggs, beaten
  1 teaspoon pure vanilla extract
 12 ounces semisweet chocolate chips

Preheat the oven to 350°F. Grease a 9 x 13-inch baking dish and set aside.

Using an electric mixer set on medium speed, combine the flour, brown sugar, butter, baking powder, salt, baking soda, eggs, and vanilla. Make sure to scrape the sides of the bowl several times while mixing. Once all of the ingredients are combined, set the mixer to slow speed and gradually add the chocolate chips. Stop mixing as soon as the chocolate chips are evenly spread throughout the batter; you don't want to mix them for too long or they will begin to break down. Spoon the batter into the prepared baking dish. Use a spatula or offset spatula to smooth the batter out so that it covers the entire dish.

Place the baking dish on the middle rack of the oven and bake the blondies for 20 to 25 minutes, or until a wooden toothpick inserted in the center of the pan comes out clean. Remove the dish from the oven and allow the blondies to cool before cutting them into individual 2 x 2-inch squares.

Blondies can be stored in an airtight container or wrapped tightly in plastic wrap for 3 days.

Fudgy Brownies

Fudgy Brownies disappear from my display case every single day without fail. Not only do customers grab these treats up, but I actually incorporate them into some of my pie recipes, such as Candy Bar Pie (page 89). You can never go wrong with this traditional treat, and I especially love this very moist and chocolaty version.

Makes approximately 2 dozen 2 x 2-inch brownies
Level: Moderate

4 ounces unsweetened chocolate, coarsely chopped
12 tablespoons (1½ sticks) salted butter
1⅓ cups unbleached all-purpose flour
½ teaspoon salt
1 teaspoon baking powder
4 large eggs, beaten
2 cups sugar
2 teaspoons pure vanilla extract
1 cup semisweet chocolate chips

Preheat the oven to 350°F. Grease a 9 x 13-inch baking pan and set aside.

In a medium saucepan, melt the chocolate and butter together over low heat, stirring constantly until smooth. Remove the saucepan from the heat and set it to the side.

In a separate bowl, combine the flour, salt, and baking powder. In a medium bowl, beat the eggs and gradually add the sugar, mixing thoroughly. Gradually add the dry mixture to the egg mixture to combine. Stir the vanilla into the chocolate mixture in the saucepan and then add the chocolate mixture to the batter, mixing them together well. Finally, add the chocolate chips, again stirring well. Pour the mixture evenly into the prepared baking pan.

Place the dish in the oven and bake for about 24 minutes, or until a toothpick inserted in the center of the brownies comes out clean. Allow the brownies to cool completely in the pan before cutting them into 2 x 2-inch squares.

Fudgy Brownies can be stored in an airtight container or wrapped tightly in plastic wrap for 3 days.

Lemon Crunch Bars

I inherited this recipe from my grandmother, who frequently attended her book and garden club meetings with Lemon Crunch Bars in tow. Indeed, these refreshing, elegant little treats are great for such gatherings and afternoon tea—whether it's an official get-together or just your own personal midday pick-me-up. These two-layer bars are very easy to make; the most time-intensive part of the process is squeezing the lemon juice.

Makes approximately 2 dozen 2 x 2-inch squares
Level: Easy

2 cups plus 2 tablespoons unbleached all-purpose flour
¾ cup confectioners' sugar
½ pound (2 sticks) salted butter, melted
2 tablespoons grated lemon zest
4 tablespoons fresh lemon juice plus (from approximately 2 lemons)
4 eggs, beaten
2 cups granulated sugar
1 teaspoon baking powder

Preheat the oven to 350°F. Grease a 9 x 13-inch baking dish and set aside.

To make the first layer of the lemon bars, in a medium bowl, sift together 2 cups of the flour and ½ cup of the confectioners' sugar. Stir the melted butter into the dry ingredients. Pack this mixture into the prepared baking dish, making sure it is evenly distributed across the dish.

Place the baking dish in the oven and bake this first layer for 15 minutes, or until the dough is slightly browned.

While the first layer is baking, prepare the second. Using an electric mixer set on

What's the Easiest Way to Juice a Lemon?

There are, of course, many ways to juice a lemon, including by hand. I'm all about saving time in any way I can without sacrificing the finished product, which is why the citrus juicer is one of my very favorite kitchen products. Citrus juicers are affordable and extremely easy to use: Just cut a lemon (or lime) in half and place one half between the two handles. Squeeze the handles down and you have a fully extracted lemon! It's very efficient and effective.

medium speed, mix together the lemon zest, lemon juice, eggs, granulated sugar, the remaining 2 tablespoons flour, and the baking powder. Be sure to scrape the sides of the bowl while mixing. Once the first layer has finished baking, pour the second layer over the top of it.

Place the dish back in the oven and bake the bars for about 25 minutes, or until they are slightly firm in the middle. Remove the pan from the oven and place it on a wire cooling rack. Allow the bars to cool completely before cutting them into 2 x 2-inch squares.

When ready to serve, sift the remaining ¼ cup confectioners' sugar over the top to garnish the bars and place each individual lemon crunch bar in a paper baking cup (be sure that you don't sift the confectioners' sugar until you're ready to garnish and serve).

Lemon Crunch Bars can be refrigerated and stored in an airtight container for 3 days.

Raspberry Bars

My customers delight in this raspberry jam and pecan cookie combination. If you like to experiment, try this recipe with different flavors of jam, such as strawberry or blueberry.

Makes approximately 2 dozen 2 x 2-inch bars
Level: Easy

2¼ cups unbleached all-purpose flour
1 cup sugar
½ pound (2 sticks) salted butter, softened
1 cup pecans, chopped into small pieces
1 egg
10 ounces seedless raspberry jam

Preheat the oven to 350°F. Grease a 9 x 13-inch baking dish and set aside.

In a medium bowl, combine the flour, sugar, and butter. Mix them together using your fingertips, until you have achieved a crumbly texture. Add the pecans, using your fingers to combine them thoroughly into the mixture. Remove 1½ cups of this mixture and set it aside (you will use this as a crumb topping). Using a wooden spoon, stir the egg into the remaining mixture.

Spread the mixture evenly across the prepared baking dish. Spread the raspberry jam across the top, extending to ½ inch from the edges of the baking dish. Sprinkle the reserved 1½ cups of crumb mixture over the raspberry jam.

Place the baking dish in the oven and bake it for about 40 minutes, or until they are golden brown. Remove the bars from the oven and allow them to cool completely before cutting them into 2 x 2-inch squares and serving.

Raspberry Bars can be stored in an airtight container at room temperature for up to 4 days.

perfect for a cup of tea

A pick-me-up cup of coffee or tea in the midafternoon generally isn't noteworthy, but accompany it with a piece of Sour Cream Coffee Cake (page 199) and that little coffee break might just be enough to brighten your whole day.

This chapter is chock-full of my favorite little day brighteners that I love keeping on hand for my family to nibble on. They're also great for entertaining. Serving up a nice cup of coffee with Cranberry-Orange Walnut Bread (page 191) will make your guests feel positively pampered, and it requires little time or preparation on your part. Many of the tea breads featured in this chapter also freeze well, which means you can keep a loaf in the freezer ready to pop out at just the right moment.

Breads and cakes are wonderful because they're so diverse. During my pregnancy I indulged in the rich Double Chocolate Bundt Cake (page 189) to satisfy frequent chocolate cravings. Blueberry-Lemon Tea Cake (page 186) and Zucchini Nut Tea Bread (page 201) are a lighter alternative, and these wonderful, flavor-filled treats can fulfill a wide variety of roles, from a sweet breakfast treat to a light dessert.

I am particularly proud of my Connecticut Specialty Food Association prizewinning Banana Tea Bread (page 182), Pumpkin Bread (page 195), and Zucchini Nut Tea Bread, all featured in this chapter. The pumpkin bread, especially, is a showstopper and one of my personal favorite desserts of any variety.

Apple Pockets

Think of an Apple Pocket as your own personal handheld apple pie. This recipe uses the same filling and crust as a traditional apple pie, but offers all of those comforting flavors in a more compact package. There's something unexpected about pocket pies that makes them feel like a very real treat. As with apple pie, Apple Pockets go great served warm with a dollop of ice cream or homemade Whipped Cream (page 228).

Makes 4 apple pockets
Level: Moderate

Crust

1 egg (for the egg wash to glaze the crust)
2 tablespoons water (for the egg wash to glaze the crust)
Dash of salt (for the egg wash to glaze the crust)
½ recipe Traditional Pastry Piecrust dough (see page 4)

Filling

¾ cup sugar
1½ tablespoons unbleached all-purpose flour
1½ teaspoons ground cinnamon
Dash of ground nutmeg
4 medium-size apples (I prefer Cortland), peeled, cored, and cut into ¼-inch slices (2 cups)
1 tablespoon salted butter, cut into 4 equal pieces

Preheat the oven to 350°F. Line a baking sheet with parchment paper and set aside.

To prepare the egg wash, in a small bowl, whisk together the egg, water, and salt. Set the egg wash aside.

Lightly sprinkle a rolling surface with flour, making sure that the entire surface is covered. Divide the disk of dough into 4 smaller disks. Roll out each small disk of dough into a circle about 7 inches in diameter. Set aside.

To prepare the filling, in a small bowl, whisk together ½ cup of the sugar, the flour, the cinnamon, and the nutmeg. Place the apples in a large bowl and sprinkle the sugar mixture over them. Toss the apples so that they are evenly coated.

Using a pastry brush, apply the egg wash to the edges of the dough circles. Measure out four ¾-cup batches of the apple mixture and place 1 batch in the center of each of the 4 dough circles. Dot each of the 4 batches of apples with 1 of the small pieces of butter. To form the pockets, fold the circle in half to enclose the apples. Using the tines of a fork, seal the edges of the circle so that the apples are completely enclosed in the dough pocket. Use a pair of kitchen scissors or a pantry knife to cut a ½-inch hole in the center of the pocket for ventilation (you can also vent the pocket with a fork if you prefer).

Place the apple pockets on the lined baking sheet. Brush the tops of the apple pockets with the remaining egg wash and sprinkle with the remaining ¼ cup sugar.

To bake, place the baking sheet on the middle rack of the oven and bake the apple pockets for 20 to 25 minutes, or until the crust turns a golden brown and the apples are tender. Insert a knife into 1 of the pockets to check the firmness of the apples. Remove the baking sheet from the oven and allow the apple pockets to cool for at least 10 minutes before serving.

Apple Pockets are best served the day they are made, but they can be kept overnight at room temperature. Serve as is or warmed with a scoop of vanilla ice cream to garnish.

Applesauce Cake

I don't think I've ever met anyone who loves entertaining quite as much as my family does. Whether it's brunch, lunch, or dinner, no event is too small to create an unbelievable spread. Applesauce Cake makes frequent appearances at these gatherings. With dried fruits and chopped nuts accenting its warm flavors, this is a good cake to serve in the fall.

Makes 1 cake, 12 to 15 slices
Level: Easy

1½ cups walnuts, chopped

1 cup chopped dates

1 cup raisins

½ teaspoon ground cinnamon

½ teaspoon ground cloves

½ teaspoon ground nutmeg

2½ cups unbleached all-purpose flour, sifted

2 teaspoons baking soda

8 tablespoons (1 stick) salted butter, softened

2 eggs

1 cup sugar

1 teaspoon pure vanilla extract

1½ cups applesauce

Preheat the oven to 350°F. Grease and flour a 9 x 3-inch Bundt pan and set aside.

In a medium bowl, combine the walnuts, dates, raisins, cinnamon, cloves, and nutmeg. Add the flour and baking soda, mixing until the nuts and dried fruit are thoroughly coated. Set the mixture aside.

Using an electric mixer set on medium speed, beat the butter, eggs, and sugar until they have achieved a light color. Stir the vanilla into the applesauce, then combine it with the ingredients in the electric mixer, again at medium speed. Pour the nuts and dried fruit mixture into the cake batter and mix on low speed. Once the ingredients are well combined, pour the batter into the Bundt pan.

Place the applesauce cake into the oven and bake it for 50 to 60 minutes, or until a wooden toothpick inserted in the center of the cake comes out clean. Allow the cake to cool for at least 30 minutes before running a knife around the edges of the cake to easily remove it from the Bundt pan. Place the cake on a wire cooling rack until it has cooled completely.

Wrap the Applesauce Cake tightly in plastic wrap to store at room temperature for up to 2 days.

Why Use a Bundt Pan?

Bundt pans are a type of tube pan. They are round, several inches deep, with a hollow tube in the middle and scalloped sides. This tube isn't just for decoration; it ensures that the cake bakes all the way through, which can be tricky with deep, moist cakes such as Applesauce Cake. Aside from their practical purpose, Bundt pans also result in a very elegant finished product. Note that fluted cake pans and Bundt pans are interchangeable.

Banana Tea Bread

Over the years I have found that people tend to have very specific ideas about which ingredients should and should not be included in Banana Tea Bread. In an effort to satisfy everyone, I carry two versions of banana bread in my store: one with chopped walnuts and one with chocolate chips. I'm sure that, just like my customers, you will also have some very distinct ideas about how banana bread is best. Although the base recipe for Banana Tea Bread always remains the same, its taste can be utterly transformed with the addition of a mere ½ cup of walnuts or chocolate chips. And, of course, if you happen to be bipartisan, you can include both walnuts and chocolate chips.

Makes 1 loaf
Level: Easy

- 8 tablespoons (1 stick) salted butter, softened
- 1 cup sugar
- 2 eggs
- 1⅓ cups ripe bananas, mashed
- 1 teaspoon whole milk
- 1 teaspoon pure vanilla extract
- 2 cups unbleached all-purpose flour
- ¼ teaspoon salt
- 1 teaspoon baking soda
- ½ cup chopped walnuts and/or ½ cup mini semisweet chocolate chips (depending upon your preference)

Preheat the oven to 350°F. Grease an 8 x 4-inch loaf pan and set aside.

To prepare the batter, using an electric mixer set on medium speed, cream the butter and sugar together until they are light and creamy. Beat the eggs in, 1 at a time. Be sure to scrape the sides of the bowl to ensure that all of the ingredients are incorporated.

In a separate medium bowl, mix together the bananas, milk, and vanilla. In another separate medium bowl, whisk together the flour, salt, and baking soda. With the mixer set on low speed, alternately add both the banana and flour mixtures to the creamed butter just until combined. Again, be sure to

Why It's Important Not to Overmix

When making tea bread, it's very important to mix ingredients only until the point where they are *just* combined. The batter may appear lumpy, but don't worry, that's okay! You want to stop mixing as soon as the dry ingredients are moistened. Overmixing will result in tough tea bread; you want your tea bread to be tender and moist.

scrape the sides of the bowl several times to incorporate all of the ingredients. If you are adding walnuts or chocolate chips, fold them into the batter. Spoon the batter into the prepared loaf pan.

To bake, place the pan in the oven and bake it for about 1 hour, or until a wooden toothpick inserted in the middle of the loaf comes out clean. Remove the bread from the oven and allow it to cool in the pan for 10 minutes. Run a knife around the edges of the loaf to easily remove it from the pan. Place the bread on a wire cooling rack to continue cooling.

Wrap the Banana Tea Bread tightly in plastic wrap to store in the refrigerator for up to 4 days. This bread also freezes well; to freeze, wrap it tightly in plastic wrap and keep it in the freezer for up to 1 month.

Blueberry Crumb Cake

The great thing about this recipe is that it's so universal. If you're a purist, omit the fruit altogether for an equally satisfying plain crumb cake. If you want to opt for something other than blueberry, apples, cranberries, and even peaches all work well in crumb cake. I recommend switching the fruit out according to what's fresh and in season, to make this cake a stupendous after-dinner treat or breakfast pick-me-up all year long. Also consider adding your favorite nuts, such as walnuts or pecans, to this cake's crumb topping.

Makes 1 cake, approximately 12 slices
Level: Easy

Topping
1   cup Cinnamon Sugar Crumb Topping (page 13)

Cake
3   cups unbleached all-purpose flour
2   cups granulated sugar
1   teaspoon baking powder
½   pound (2 sticks) salted butter
2   eggs
¾   cup whole milk
1   teaspoon pure vanilla extract
3   cups blueberries, fresh or frozen (I prefer fresh)
¼   cup confectioners' sugar

Preheat the oven to 350°F. Grease and flour a 9 x 13-inch baking dish and set aside.

To prepare the batter, in a medium bowl, combine the flour, granulated sugar, and baking powder. Use a pastry blender to blend the butter into the flour mixture until it forms pea-size pieces. Remove 1½ cups of the flour mixture and add it to the cinnamon sugar crumb topping and toss well to fully combine.

Transfer the remaining flour mixture to the bowl of an electric mixer set on medium speed and add the eggs, milk, and vanilla. Mix until combined. Fold the blueberries into the cake batter. Spoon the cake batter into the prepared baking dish. Sprinkle the crumb topping over the batter.

To bake, place the baking dish on a baking sheet and place the sheet on the middle rack of the oven. Bake the cake for 45 to 50 minutes, or until a wooden toothpick inserted in the center of the cake comes out clean. Remove the baking dish from the oven and allow the cake to cool for at least 1 hour before serving.

To serve, dust the top of the cake with sifted confectioners' sugar.

Blueberry Crumb Cake can be stored at room temperature for up to 2 days when wrapped tightly with plastic wrap.

Blueberry-Lemon Tea Cake

Have you ever gone blueberry picking only to find that you don't know what to do with all those scrumptious blueberries once you get them home? Enter Blueberry-Lemon Tea Cake (which, by the way, is also delicious with frozen blueberries). The combination of tangy lemon and blueberry is just as bright as a summer's day. This light but satisfying treat is great for brunches or picnic lunches during the warmer months. Be sure to take the final step and add the lemon glaze to this tea cake; the extra three minutes are definitely worth the effort!

Makes 1 loaf, 8 to 10 slices
Level: Easy

Cake

  6   tablespoons (¾ stick) salted butter, softened
1⅓   cups sugar
  2   eggs
  2   tablespoons grated lemon zest (from 2 lemons)
  ¼   cup fresh lemon juice (from 2 lemons)
1½   cups unbleached all-purpose flour
  1   teaspoon baking powder
  ¼   teaspoon salt
  ¾   cup whole milk
1¼   cups blueberries, fresh or frozen (I prefer fresh)

Glaze

  3   tablespoons fresh lemon juice (from 1 to 2 lemons)
  ⅓   cup sugar, plus 2 tablespoons sugar, for garnish (optional)

Preheat the oven to 350°F. Grease and flour an 8 x 4-inch loaf pan and set aside.

Using an electric mixer set on medium speed, beat the butter until it achieves a creamy consistency. Gradually add the sugar and continue beating until the mixture becomes light and fluffy. Add the eggs, 1 at a time. Add the lemon zest and lemon juice, continuing to blend until all of the ingredients are well combined.

In a separate bowl, whisk together the flour, baking powder, and salt, then add it to the lemon mixture in the electric mixer. Slowly add the milk while beating on low speed until it's thoroughly incorporated. Fold in the fresh blueberries. Spoon the batter into the prepared loaf pan.

Bake the cake for 50 to 60 minutes, or until a wooden toothpick inserted in the center of the tea cake comes out clean. Remove the tea cake from the oven and allow it to cool in the pan for about 15 minutes. Run a knife around the edges of the tea cake to easily remove it from the pan. Place it on a wire cooling rack set over a sheet tray to continue cooling for 20 to 30 minutes. While the tea cake is still slightly warm, begin to prepare the glaze.

To prepare the glaze, in a small saucepan off of the heat, combine the lemon juice and ⅓ cup sugar. Place the saucepan over medium heat and stir constantly for about 3 minutes, or until the sugar dissolves. Remove the glaze from the heat and immediately pour it over the tea cake. If you would like a final sweet-and-sour finish, you can also combine the lemon zest with 2 tablespoons of sugar and sprinkle them over the top of the glaze.

Blueberry-Lemon Tea Cake is best eaten immediately, but you can also wrap it tightly in plastic wrap to store at room temperature for up to 2 days.

Double Chocolate Bundt Cake

Double Chocolate Bundt Cake has been another lifesaver for pregnancy chocolate cravings. Although I make this cake to satisfy my own need for chocolate, it's also the one type of cake that my husband is pretty much guaranteed to hoard: It's survival of the fittest in my house when Double Chocolate Bundt Cake is up for offer! Not only does this cake use chocolate as the foundation of the batter, but it also incorporates chocolate chips for that extra-layered punch of chocolate. Be sure to eat Double Chocolate Bundt Cake warm to maximize its satisfying chocolate richness.

Makes 1 cake, 12 to 15 slices
Level: Moderate

    5 ounces unsweetened chocolate, chopped
1½ cups granulated sugar
 12 tablespoons (1½ sticks) salted butter, softened
    4 eggs, separated
1½ cups cake flour
    2 teaspoons baking powder
  ½ teaspoon ground cinnamon
    1 cup whole milk
    1 teaspoon pure vanilla extract
    1 cup semisweet chocolate chips

Garnish
Chocolate Ganache (page 224), warm
  ¼ cup confectioners' sugar

Preheat the oven to 325°F. Grease and flour a 9 x 3-inch Bundt pan.

In a double boiler over high heat, melt the unsweetened chocolate until it's smooth, stirring frequently. Set it aside to cool.

Using an electric mixer set on medium speed, cream together the granulated sugar and butter until the mixture becomes light in color. Set the egg whites aside and add the egg yolks, again on medium speed.

In a separate small bowl, sift together the cake flour, baking powder, and cinnamon.

Add half of the sifted flour mixture to the butter-sugar mixture and mix on low speed until they are just combined (it's important not to overmix). Add half of the milk and mix again until just combined. Repeat again, adding the second half of the sifted flour mixture and the remaining milk, continuing to take care not to overmix the batter.

On low speed, add the melted chocolate and the vanilla. Finally, add the chocolate chips and mix until they are thoroughly combined. Set the mixture aside.

In a separate medium bowl, beat the egg whites until they become stiff. Fold the beaten egg whites into the cake batter until all of the ingredients are combined. Spoon the batter into the Bundt pan.

To bake, place the Bundt pan on a baking sheet on the middle rack of the oven and bake the cake for 45 to 50 minutes, or until a wooden toothpick inserted in the center of the cake comes out clean. Remove the cake from the oven and allow it to cool in the pan for 15 minutes. Run a knife around the edges of the cake to easily remove it from the pan. Place it on a wire cooling rack to cool for at least 1 hour more.

Pour the warm ganache over the cake just before serving. Dust the ganache with the confectioners' sugar.

If you have not yet garnished the cake with ganache and confectioners' sugar, Double Chocolate Bundt Cake can be covered tightly with plastic wrap and kept overnight at room temperature. If the ganache has been poured over the cake, place the cake in the refrigerator to store for up to 3 days.

Cranberry-Orange Walnut Bread

Cranberry-Orange Walnut Bread is in constant rotation at my house in the autumn months. I like to include walnuts, for the simple fact that they provide a bit of additional texture to this bread. This recipe works perfectly well without the walnuts, though, so feel free to omit them if that's your preference. The orange provides natural sweetness, but if you like things a little sweeter, sprinkle some Cinnamon Sugar Crumb Topping (page 13) on top of the bread just before baking. If you enjoy starting your day with muffins, this recipe can easily be transformed; follow all directions as provided for the bread, fill the muffin cups to two thirds of the way full, and shorten the baking time to twenty to twenty-five minutes.

Makes 1 loaf, 10 to 12 slices
Level: Easy

2 eggs
¾ cup whole milk
½ cup vegetable oil
¾ cup sugar
2 cups plus 2 tablespoons unbleached all-purpose flour
1 tablespoon baking powder
½ teaspoon salt
¾ teaspoon ground cinnamon
¼ teaspoon ground nutmeg
1 tablespoon grated orange zest (from about 1 orange)
1 cup whole cranberries, fresh or frozen
¼ cup chopped walnuts

Preheat the oven to 350°F. Grease and flour an 8 x 4-inch loaf pan and set aside.

Using an electric mixer set on medium speed, combine the eggs, milk, vegetable oil, and sugar. Once they are combined, add the flour, baking powder, salt, cinnamon, nutmeg, and orange zest. Being careful not to overmix, mix again on medium speed until the ingredients are just combined. Add the cranberries and walnuts and mix on low speed. Spoon the batter into the prepared loaf pan.

Place the pan on the middle rack of the oven and bake for 60 to 65 minutes, or until a wooden toothpick inserted in the middle of the bread comes out clean. Remove the bread from the oven and allow it to cool in the pan for at least 10 minutes. Run a knife around the edges of the loaf to easily remove it from the pan. Place it on a wire cooling rack to finish cooling.

Cranberry-Orange Walnut Bread can be served immediately or, once completely cooled, wrapped tightly in plastic wrap and kept in the refrigerator for up to 4 days. This bread can also be stored in the freezer for up to 1 month.

Maple Pecan Cake

As a child of New England, I have always had maple syrup at my fingertips. Growing up, I took it for granted; but once I got a bit older I began to truly appreciate that great maple taste, whether it was delivered on top of my pancakes or as the foundation of a dessert dish. As you can tell by this cookbook, I love incorporating maple into my own creations. It always takes me back to those early days of Michele's Pies, when the business was run out of my tiny kitchen in Vermont, home state of all things maple. As always, I prefer to use Grade B pure Vermont maple syrup for this cake, but Grade A will also work. If you're a real maple nut, be sure to top this cake with Maple Whipped Cream (page 229).

Makes 1 cake, approximately 12 slices
Level: Moderate

2 cups pecan halves
3 cups sugar
3 cups unbleached all-purpose flour
1 teaspoon baking powder
½ pound (2 sticks) salted butter, cold, plus 2 tablespoons salted butter, melted
5 eggs
1 cup whole milk
2 teaspoons pure vanilla extract
1 cup Grade B pure Vermont maple syrup (you can also use Grade A)

Preheat the oven to 350°F. Grease a 9 x 13-inch baking pan and set aside.

To toast the pecan halves, place the pecans on a baking sheet and bake them for 5 minutes. Leaving the oven on, remove the pecans from the oven and set them aside while you begin making the batter.

To prepare the batter, in a large bowl, combine 2 cups of the sugar, the flour, the baking powder, and the cold butter. Using a pastry blender, cut the butter into pea-size pieces. Place this mixture in the bowl of an electric mixer, then add 2 of the eggs, the milk, and 1 teaspoon of the vanilla. Begin to mix on medium speed until all of the ingredients are just combined; be sure not to overmix. Set the batter aside.

In a separate medium bowl, on medium speed, mix together the maple syrup, the 3 remaining eggs, the melted butter, the remaining 1 teaspoon vanilla, and the remaining 1 cup sugar. Mix until all of the ingredients are well combined. Using a spatula, fold this maple syrup mixture into the cake batter and mix well. Finally, fold in the toasted pecan halves. Pour the batter into the prepared baking pan.

To bake, place the pan on the middle rack of the oven and bake for 50 to 55 minutes, or until a wooden toothpick inserted in the center of the cake comes out clean. Remove the baking pan from the oven and allow the cake to cool for at least 30 minutes.

Maple Pecan Cake can be stored at room temperature for up to 3 days when tightly covered in plastic wrap.

Pumpkin Bread

No matter how hard I try to keep up, every single autumn my customers buy up all of my shop's Connecticut Specialty Food Association prize-winning pumpkin bread more quickly than I can stock it. I understand—it's my favorite bread too! I've said it before and I'll say it again: A big part of what makes this bread and all of Michele's Pies' other pumpkin treats so special is that I use fresh pumpkin puree. In the case of Pumpkin Bread, this makes for a perfectly moist bread. If you have a bit of extra time to spare, I recommend you do the same (see page 51 for instructions on puree-ing your own pumpkin). If you're in a hurry, store-bought pumpkin will also work. This recipe yields three loaves of pumpkin bread, so if you don't have three loaf pans on hand, feel free to use disposable tins. Alternatively, you can make muffins with the extra batter by filling the muffin cups two-thirds of the way and baking for twenty to twenty-five minutes, or until a toothpick inserted in the center comes out clean.

Makes 3 large loaves
Level: Easy

3 cups sugar

1 cup vegetable oil

4 eggs

3¼ cups unbleached all purpose flour

2 teaspoons baking soda

1½ teaspoons salt

1½ teaspoons ground cinnamon

¾ teaspoon ground nutmeg

⅔ cup water

16 ounces pumpkin puree

Preheat the oven to 350°F. Grease three 8 x 4-inch loaf pans and set them aside.

To prepare the batter, using an electric mixer set on medium speed, beat together the sugar and vegetable oil. Add the eggs, 1 at a time. Be sure to scrape the sides of the bowl with a spatula to ensure that all of the ingredients are incorporated. Set the bowl aside.

In a medium bowl, whisk together the flour, baking soda, salt, cinnamon, and nutmeg. Alternate adding the whisked dry ingredients and the water to the batter and beat on medium speed. After each addition, scrape the sides of the bowl so that all of the ingredients are incorporated. Finally, turn the electric mixer down to low and add the pumpkin puree until completely incorporated. Evenly divide the batter among the 3 prepared loaf pans.

To bake, place the loaf pans in the oven and bake them for 45 to 50 minutes, or until a wooden toothpick inserted in the center of the bread comes out clean. Allow the bread to cool in the loaf pans for 10 to 15 minutes. Run a knife around the edges of each loaf to easily remove it from the pan. Place the loaves on a wire cooling rack to continue cooling.

Wrap the Pumpkin Bread tightly in plastic wrap to store in the refrigerator for up to 4 days. This bread also freezes well; to freeze, wrap it tightly in plastic wrap and keep it in the freezer for up to 1 month.

Sour Cream Coffee Cake

My mom used to make Sour Cream Coffee Cake to serve with coffee or tea at the end of a meal. What I most looked forward to, though, were the leftovers we'd have for breakfast the next day. This is a great basic coffee cake recipe that doesn't utilize any extras like nuts or raisins. However, you should feel free to customize it to your own preferences; if you fancy chopped nuts or raisins, just add them as the final step of preparing the brown sugar topping.

Makes 1 cake, approximately 12 slices
Level: Easy

Cake
8   tablespoons (1 stick) salted butter
1   cup granulated sugar
2   eggs
2   cups unbleached all-purpose flour
1   teaspoon baking soda
1   teaspoon baking powder
1   teaspoon pure vanilla extract
8   ounces sour cream

Brown Sugar Topping
⅓   cup firmly packed dark brown sugar
¾   teaspoon ground cinnamon
6   tablespoons (¾ stick) salted butter, softened

Garnish (optional)
¼   cup confectioners' sugar, sifted

Preheat the oven to 375°F. Grease and flour a 9 x 3-inch Bundt pan and set aside.

To prepare the batter, using an electric mixer set on medium speed, cream the butter and the granulated sugar until they become light in color, about 2 minutes. Add the eggs and mix again. Add the flour, baking soda, baking powder, vanilla, and sour cream, continuing to mix on medium speed. Be sure to scrape the sides of the bowl and continue mixing until the ingredients are just combined, being careful not to overmix. Spoon the batter evenly across the prepared Bundt pan. Set the pan aside.

To prepare the topping, place the brown sugar and cinnamon in a small bowl. Using a pastry blender, cut the butter into the dry ingredients until the butter is in pea-size pieces. Sprinkle the brown sugar mixture evenly across the batter in the Bundt pan. Use a dull knife to swirl the brown sugar mixture into the batter as evenly as possible.

Place the Bundt pan on a baking sheet and place the sheet on the middle rack of the oven. Bake the cake for 40 to 45 minutes, or until a wooden toothpick inserted in the center of the cake comes out clean. Remove the cake from the oven and allow it to cool in the pan for 15 minutes. Run a knife around the edges of the cake to easily remove it from the pan. Place it on a wire cooling rack to continue cooling.

Once the cake has cooled completely, dust the top with confectioners' sugar, if desired, and serve.

Wrap the Sour Cream Coffee Cake tightly in plastic wrap to store at room temperature for up to 2 days.

Zucchini Nut Tea Bread

Generally speaking, I'm an advocate of exercising honesty with kids. However, there is one little secret that I do keep from my son Dakota. That "summer bread" he loves so much? It has zucchini in it, and Dakota is none the wiser. It always makes me chuckle a bit when he turns his nose up at zucchini served as a vegetable with dinner, yet can't get enough of this bread for dessert. Be sure to strain the zucchini well to remove as much water as possible.

Makes 1 loaf
Level: Easy

3 eggs
2 cups sugar
1 cup vegetable oil
1 tablespoon pure vanilla extract
2 cups unbleached all-purpose flour
2 cups grated and strained zucchini
2 teaspoons baking soda
1 teaspoon salt
½ teaspoon baking powder
1 tablespoon ground cinnamon
1 cup chopped walnuts

Preheat the oven to 350°F. Grease and flour an 8 x 4-inch loaf pan and set aside.

To prepare the batter, using an electric mixer set on medium speed, beat together the eggs, sugar, and vegetable oil. Once combined, add the vanilla, flour, zucchini, baking soda, salt, baking powder, and cinnamon and continue mixing on medium speed until all of the ingredients are just incorporated, being careful not to overmix. Turn the mixer down to low speed, and mix in the walnuts. Scrape the sides of the bowl to make sure all of the ingredients are well incorporated. Spoon the batter into the prepared loaf pan.

Place the tea bread in the oven and bake for 50 to 60 minutes, or until a wooden toothpick inserted in the center of the tea bread comes out clean. Allow the tea bread to cool in the pan for 10 minutes. Run a knife around the edges of the tea bread to easily remove it from the pan. Place the tea bread on a wire cooling rack to continue cooling.

Wrap the Zucchini Nut Tea Bread tightly in plastic wrap to store in the refrigerator for up to 4 days. This tea bread also freezes well; to freeze, wrap it tightly in plastic wrap and keep it in the freezer for up to 1 month.

lovin' spoonful

In my family, one of the ways we express our love for one another is through food. The recipes in this chapter really epitomize that sentiment for me.

Included in this chapter are desserts that will warm up you and your loved ones from the inside out. I love serving Apple Crisp (page 206), Bread Pudding (page 211), or Old-Fashioned Baked Rice Pudding (page 215) to my husband and son, Dakota, on chilly fall nights. For me, providing these warm dishes and filling the house with comforting aromas in the process is just another way of saying, "I love you."

Even though there's no need to warm up in the summertime, for me, the more fruit-based recipes in this chapter are the summer equivalent of comfort foods. Peach-Blueberry Cobbler (page 213) and Strawberry Shortcake (page 217) share that same special homegrown quality that makes the warmer recipes in this chapter so appealing.

I am a firm believer that food should not only taste good—it should make you and those you love *feel* good, too. There's no doubt that the lovin' spoonfuls in this chapter do exactly that.

Apple Crisp

My grandmother's dear friend Della shared her family's apple crisp recipe with my grandmother many, many years ago. Since then, it's become *my* family's go-to apple crisp recipe as well. This version of apple crisp is simple but perfect, incorporating just the right amount of spices and heft to make this classic treat sing. Apple crisp is best when served warm with vanilla ice cream.

Makes one 9 x 9-inch pan of crisp; approximately 8 servings
Level: Easy

Filling
- ¾ cup sugar
- 2 tablespoons ground cinnamon
- Dash of ground nutmeg
- 2 tablespoons unbleached all-purpose flour
- 8 to 10 Cortland, Granny Smith, or Crispin apples, peeled, cored, and cut into ½-inch cubes (about 10 cups)

Topping
- 1 cup unbleached all-purpose flour
- 1 cup quick-cooking rolled oats
- 2 teaspoons ground cinnamon
- 1 teaspoon ground nutmeg
- ¼ teaspoon salt
- 8 tablespoons (1 stick) salted butter, slightly softened

Preheat the oven to 400°F. Grease a 9 x 9-inch baking dish and set aside.

To prepare the filling, in a small bowl, whisk together the sugar, cinnamon, nutmeg, and flour. Place the apples in a large bowl and pour the dry ingredients over them.

Toss the apples to evenly coat. Spoon the apples into the prepared baking dish.

To prepare the topping, in a medium bowl, combine the flour, oats, cinnamon, nutmeg, and salt. Using a pastry blender, cut the butter into the dry ingredients until the butter is the size of peas. Sprinkle the topping evenly over the apple filling.

Place the baking dish on a baking sheet and put the baking sheet on the middle rack of the oven. Bake the crisp for 15 minutes. Reduce the heat to 350°F and continue baking for about another 30 minutes, or until the top is nicely browned and crisp and the apples are tender when tested with a knife.

Allow the apple crisp to cool for 10 to 15 minutes before serving warm with a dollop of vanilla ice cream or whipped cream.

Apple Crisp can be stored in the refrigerator for up to 2 days when covered tightly with plastic wrap.

Blueberry-Blackberry Turnovers

Although most of us automatically associate turnovers with apples, there's no need to limit them to this single fruit. Great for either breakfast or dessert, not only are Blueberry-Blackberry Turnovers unique and easy to make, but you will also have the pleasure of seeing a look of delighted surprise cross the faces of your friends and family members when they bite into this turnover and find fresh berries. At the height of summer when blackberries and blueberries are abundant, just purchase some puff pastry from your local grocery store and you're ready to go. This recipe also works well with apples, blueberries, or a combination of strawberries and rhubarb. To experiment, just use the recipe for your favorite fruit pie filling and divide it among the turnovers as explained here.

Makes 4 turnovers
Level: Easy

1 cup sugar

⅓ cup unbleached all-purpose flour

½ teaspoon ground cinnamon

2 cups fresh blueberries, washed and dried

2 cups fresh blackberries, washed and dried

2 eggs

2 tablespoons water

4 6 x 6-inch puff pastry squares, thawed

2 tablespoons salted butter, divided into 4 pieces

Preheat the oven to 400°F. Line a baking sheet with parchment paper and set aside.

To prepare the filling, in a medium bowl, whisk together ¾ cup of the sugar, the flour, and the cinnamon. Add the blueberries and blackberries and gently toss them with the dry ingredients until the berries are completely coated.

To prepare the egg wash, crack the eggs into a small bowl, add the water, and whisk. Set the egg wash aside.

On the lined baking sheet, place the 4 puff pastry squares at least 2 inches apart. Spoon 1 cup of the berry mixture into the middle of each of the 4 puff pastry squares. Dot each batch of fruit filling with 1 of the butter pieces. Using a pastry brush, brush the 2 opposite corners of the puff pastry with the egg wash. Turn both corners inward so that they meet in the middle of the berries. Make sure that the 2 corners are pinched together well so they don't come apart while baking. Brush the entire surface of the turnovers with the egg wash. Sprinkle the remaining ¼ cup sugar across the 4 turnovers.

Place the baking sheet on the middle rack of the oven and bake for about 20 minutes, or until the turnovers are golden brown and the fruit is bubbling.

Blueberry-Blackberry Turnovers are best served the same day or can be warmed in the oven for 5 minutes at 350°F before serving. I like to serve turnovers topped off with Whipped Cream (see page 228) or vanilla ice cream.

Bread Pudding

Bread Pudding is one of those time-tested comfort foods that stirs up a sense of nostalgia. It's a simple but satisfying treat that doesn't require much more than basic ingredients you likely have on hand in your kitchen. It's a great way to use up leftover bread, since day-old bread will absorb better than fresh bread will.

There are so many variations of bread pudding, but I've found that most of my customers favor a raisin medley with dried cranberries. You can easily substitute chopped apples or even pears for the raisins and cranberries. If you want your guests to think you slaved away for hours on this dessert, drizzle my vanilla sauce over the bread pudding before serving. I prefer my bread pudding slightly warmed with the vanilla sauce, but I know others who prefer it cold. If you run out of time, you can even serve this bread pudding warmed and drizzled with some heavy cream. That's the beauty of this dish: Anything goes!

Makes 8 servings
Level: Easy

Bread Pudding

10 cups day-old bread cubes (I prefer challah, but any white bread or soft dinner roll will work)
 5 cups whole milk, warmed
 1 cup granulated sugar
 1 teaspoon ground nutmeg
 2 teaspoons ground cinnamon
 2 teaspoons pure vanilla extract
 1 cup raisin medley (a mixture of dark and golden raisins)
 1 cup dried cranberries
 8 large eggs, beaten

Vanilla Sauce (optional)

½ cup granulated sugar

½ cup firmly packed dark brown sugar

8 tablespoons (1 stick) salted butter

¾ cup heavy cream

Preheat the oven to 375°F. Grease a 9 x 13-inch baking dish.

Place the bread cubes in the prepared baking dish. Pour the warm milk over the bread and stir so that the bread absorbs the milk.

In a medium bowl, combine the granulated sugar, nutmeg, cinnamon, and vanilla. Add the raisins and dried cranberries to the dry mixture and toss until they are evenly coated. Add the beaten eggs to the raisin mixture and mix thoroughly. Add the raisin mixture to the bread, folding it in so that it's evenly combined throughout the baking dish.

To bake, place the baking dish in a water bath (see page 216) on the middle rack of the oven and bake for about 45 minutes, or until the bread is slightly puffed and the top is dry to the touch. Remove the bread pudding from the oven and let it set for at least 15 minutes before serving.

In the meantime, make the vanilla sauce if using. In a medium saucepan over medium heat, stir and heat the granulated sugar, brown sugar, butter, and heavy cream until the butter is melted and all of the ingredients are combined. Bring the sauce to a boil, then turn off the heat.

Serve the bread pudding in individual dishes or bowls garnished with the vanilla sauce.

Bread Pudding can be kept in the refrigerator for up to 3 days when wrapped tightly with plastic wrap.

Peach-Blueberry Cobbler

If you love pie but want to try something a bit different, Peach-Blueberry Cobbler is the way to go. Like pies, cobblers are comprised of a fruit filling and top crust (in this case lattice-style); the difference is that the fruit filling in cobblers is inserted directly into the baking dish, without a pie shell. For me, peaches and blueberries perfectly capture the essence of summer, but this is another one of those recipes where you should feel free to mix it up and experiment. If you choose to do this, I recommend selecting whatever fruits happen to be the ripest and most flavorful at any given time: Perhaps you may want to give raspberries, strawberries, or blackberries a whirl. For an extra treat, serve this cobbler warm with vanilla ice cream.

Makes 9 servings
Level: Moderate

6 cups peaches, peeled, pitted, and sliced into ½-inch slices (8 to 10 peaches)
2 cups fresh blueberries
1 tablespoon fresh lemon juice
1 cup plus 2 tablespoons sugar
3 tablespoons quick-cooking tapioca
3 tablespoons cornstarch
2 tablespoons firmly packed dark brown sugar
   Pinch of salt
½ recipe Traditional Pastry Piecrust dough (see page 4)
2 tablespoons heavy cream

Preheat the oven to 375°F. Grease an 8 x 8-inch baking dish.

In a medium bowl, gently mix together the peaches and blueberries. Sprinkle the lemon juice over the fruit and gently mix again. Set the fruit aside.

In a small bowl, whisk together 1 cup of the sugar, the tapioca, the cornstarch, the brown sugar, and the salt. Sprinkle the dry mixture over the peaches and blueberries and toss gently until the fruit is covered. Spoon the fruit mixture into the prepared baking dish. Set the dish aside.

Lightly sprinkle a rolling surface with flour, making sure that the entire surface is covered. Roll out the pie dough to about ¼-inch thickness. Using a sharp knife or a pastry wheel, cut the dough into ¾-inch strips. Place the strips over the top of the fruit, lattice-style, so that the edges of the strips meet the edges of the baking dish. Ultimately, you want to create a checkerboard effect, with the lattice strips placed both vertically and horizontally across the fruit, weaving the dough strips in and out in an over-under pattern. Trim any edges of extra dough hanging over the baking dish so that the lattice strips are flush with the sides of the dish. Brush the lattice top with the heavy cream and sprinkle the remaining ⅛ cup of sugar over the top.

Place the cobbler on the middle rack of the oven and bake for 50 to 55 minutes, or until the fruit is bubbly and the crust is golden brown. Remove the cobbler from the oven and place the dish on a wire cooling rack to cool.

Peach-Blueberry Cobbler can be kept at room temperature for up to 2 days or stored in the refrigerator for up to 4 days.

Old-Fashioned Baked Rice Pudding

My father-in-law, Doug, inspired this rice pudding recipe; both he and my husband, Kelly, swear that this is the only traditional way to make it. Before meeting the Stuarts, I always thought of rice pudding as a creamy stovetop treat, but they are adamant that it must be baked, which makes for a denser pudding. All it took was one taste of Doug's baked rice pudding to sway me over to their camp. My family prefers rice pudding with raisins, which are included in this recipe. You can feel free to omit the raisins altogether or substitute them with your favorite dried fruit (I particularly like dried blueberries and dried cherries). I recommend using Arborio rice, as the shorter grain makes for a creamy texture. Rice pudding can be served either warm or cold, depending upon your preference. Garnish it with Whipped Cream (page 228) or heavy cream to add that extra special touch.

Makes 5 cups
Level: Moderate

3 cups rice (preferably Arborio rice)

3 cups whole milk

2 teaspoons pure vanilla extract

1 tablespoon salted butter

½ teaspoon salt

½ teaspoon ground nutmeg

1 teaspoon ground cinnamon

1 cup raisins (optional)

4 eggs

1¼ cups sugar

½ cup heavy cream

½ cup half-and-half

Why Use a Water Bath?

Water baths are used to ensure delicate foods are not overcooked during the baking process. Creating a water bath is very simple: Just place the pan containing your baked good into a larger baking pan. Pour enough water into the larger pan to come about halfway up the sides of the smaller pan. Surrounding the smaller pan with water ensures that the temperature of the baked good is insulated, since the water temperature will not rise above 212°F. This means the sides of the smaller pan will not be exposed to high heat, yet the middle of the baked good will cook through. This ultimately provides a smooth, even texture and guards against any curdling.

To prepare the rice, follow the rice cooking directions, except you will omit the water and instead use the whole milk. Add 1 teaspoon of the vanilla, the butter, and the salt. Cook according to the directions, until the rice is tender.

Preheat the oven to 350°F.

Stir the nutmeg and cinnamon into the rice. If you are adding raisins, stir them in. Allow the rice to cool.

When the rice has cooled, in a large oven-safe bowl, whisk together the eggs, 1 cup of the sugar, the heavy cream, the half-and-half, and the remaining teaspoon of vanilla. Once all of the ingredients are thoroughly combined, add the seasoned rice to the bowl and stir until the rice is evenly coated.

To bake, place the bowl in a water bath on the middle rack of the oven and bake the rice pudding for 25 minutes. Remove the bowl from the oven and sprinkle the remaining ¼ cup of sugar over the top of the rice pudding. Continue to bake for about 25 minutes more, or until a knife inserted in the center of the pudding comes out clean.

Allow the rice pudding to cool before serving or storing it in the refrigerator.

Old-Fashioned Baked Rice Pudding can be refrigerated for 3 days when covered tightly in plastic wrap.

Strawberry Shortcake

Over the years I've found that I simply can't stock enough strawberry shortcake to satisfy farmer's market customers. At the height of summer, when fresh strawberries are at their sweetest, it seems there is an almost insatiable desire for this fresh, light treat comprised of strawberries, homemade biscuit, and whipped cream. In this version, the strawberries are macerated in Grand Marnier, a liqueur that carries hints of orange. Note that for best results Strawberry Shortcake should be served immediately.

Makes 7 strawberry shortcakes
Level: Moderate

¾ cup sugar

1¾ cups unbleached all-purpose flour

1 tablespoon baking powder

¾ teaspoon salt

½ cup vegetable shortening (such as Crisco)

⅓ cup whole milk

1 egg

8 cups fresh strawberries, washed and hulled, plus 7 strawberries (for garnish)

1 tablespoon Grand Marnier (or to taste)

3 cups Whipped Cream (page 228)

Preheat the oven to 425°F. Line a baking sheet with parchment paper and set aside.

To prepare the biscuits, in a medium bowl, whisk together ¼ cup of the sugar, the flour, the baking powder, and the salt. Using a pastry blender, cut the vegetable shortening into the dry mixture until the shortening is the size of peas. Add the milk and egg and use your fingertips to gently and gradually form the dough into a ball. Separate the dough into ¼-cup sections and roll them into individual balls, then flatten them into a biscuit shape using your palm. Place them at least 2 inches apart on the lined baking sheet, as the dough will expand in the oven.

To bake the biscuits, place the baking sheet on the middle rack of the oven and bake for 10 to 12 minutes, or until the biscuits turn golden brown and are firm in the middle. Allow the biscuits to cool completely (for about 20 minutes) before assembling the shortcake.

You can prepare the strawberries while the biscuits are baking. In a medium bowl, using a pastry blender, mash the strawberries with the remaining ½ cup sugar until the strawberries are in small pieces and there are lots of juices. Add the Grand Marnier and mix well. Cover the bowl tightly with plastic wrap and allow the strawberry mixture to sit while the biscuits bake and cool.

To assemble the shortcake, cut 1 biscuit in half. Place the bottom half of the biscuit on an individual serving dish or bowl and scoop ¾ cup of the strawberry mixture on top of the biscuit half. Place the second half of the biscuit on top of the strawberries. Top the biscuit with a large dollop of whipped cream. Garnish the whipped cream with a strawberry and serve immediately.

top this

Think of the sauces, glazes, and garnishes in this chapter as the bow on a beautiful present—the final touches that complete your baking creations. After all the effort you've put into making delicious desserts, why not take that last step to ensure that they are nothing short of perfect? A homemade pie garnished with store-bought whipped cream is great. A homemade pie garnished with homemade whipped cream is an event! You'll be amazed at what a difference the addition of the homemade toppings in this chapter make to your baking repertoire. Your guests will immediately notice that there is something very, very special about your pies and sweet treats.

Not only will the finishing touches in this chapter complement the desserts included throughout this cookbook but, more generally, many of them are also great to have on hand in the kitchen. Hot Fudge Sauce (page 223) and Caramel Sauce (page 222), for example, will keep in the refrigerator for weeks. With these simple garnishes, you can add a delicious homemade touch to even a simple bowl of vanilla ice cream after dinner.

You'll also find several variations of whipped creams in this chapter. I can't stress how simple whipped cream is to make and how very much worth the few extra minutes it is. Whipped cream is also very versatile. The addition of just a little bit of flavoring will create a completely unique taste. If you feel like experimenting, just add some flavoring to the basic recipe for Whipped Cream (page 228) and see what wonderful tastes you can create.

Caramel Sauce

Caramel Sauce must be refrigerated for at least five hours prior to use, so be sure to prepare it ahead of time. Try this with Apple Caramel Crunch Pie (page 18) and Turtle Pecan Pie (page 99).

Makes 1½ cups

⅓ cup water

1½ cups sugar

1 tablespoon salted butter

1½ cups heavy cream

1 teaspoon pure vanilla extract

In a medium, heavy-bottomed saucepan, combine the water and sugar over low heat. Continue heating until the sugar dissolves, 6 to 8 minutes. Once the sugar has dissolved, increase the heat and bring the mixture to a boil, letting it boil until it turns brown. (Do not stir or whisk the mixture while it is boiling. You may, however, brush down the sides of the saucepan with a pastry brush that has been dipped in water.) When the mixture has browned, add the butter and then gradually add the heavy cream and then the vanilla. Stir the ingredients occasionally until the caramel dissolves and the sauce is thick and smooth. Pour the caramel sauce into a covered bowl. Once cooled, refrigerate for at least 5 hours.

Caramel Sauce can be kept refrigerated in an airtight container for several weeks.

Hot Fudge Sauce

Hot Fudge Sauce will need to cool and thicken for at least five hours prior to serving, so be sure to leave plenty of lead time. Try this with Graham Cracker Cream Fluff Pie (page 65), Chocolate Silk Pie (page 63), or Thin Mint Chocolate Cookie Pie (page 116).

Makes 4 cups

1 cup sugar

3 cups heavy cream

¼ cup light corn syrup (such as Karo)

4 ounces unsweetened chocolate, chopped

4 tablespoons (½ stick) salted butter

1 tablespoon pure vanilla extract

In a medium saucepan, combine the sugar, heavy cream, corn syrup, chocolate, and butter over medium-high heat until the mixture begins to bubble. Keep the pan over the heat and cook, whisking constantly, for about 5 minutes, or until the sauce looks as though it's separating. Remove the sauce from the heat and add the vanilla. Transfer the fudge sauce to a heat-proof dish or container and allow it to cool a bit before placing it in the refrigerator. Chill the sauce until it thickens, for at least 5 hours.

Hot Fudge Sauce can be kept refrigerated in an airtight container for about 2 weeks.

Chocolate Ganache

Try this with Almond Joy Pie (page 87), Double Chocolate Bundt Cake (page 189), Chocolate-Strawberry Napoleon Pie (page 112), and Strawberry Napoleon Layer Pie (page 129).

Makes 2 cups

1 cups semisweet chocolate chips
1 cup heavy cream

Place the chocolate chips in a medium, heat-proof glass bowl and set it aside. In a small saucepan over high heat, bring the heavy cream to a boil. Remove from the heat. Pour the heavy cream over the chocolate chips and mix vigorously, until the chocolate chips are melted into the cream. Allow the ganache to cool to room temperature before refrigerating.

Chocolate Ganache will keep for up to 2 weeks when stored in the refrigerator. To reheat, place the ganache in a microwave-safe container and microwave for about 1 minute, stirring every 30 seconds until warmed.

perfect pies & more

Glacé

Try Blackberry Glacé with Key Lime–Blackberry Chiffon Pie (page 119) and Lemon Chess Pie (page 36); Raspberry Glacé with Lemon-Raspberry Twist Pie (page 121); and Strawberry Glacé with Chocolate-Strawberry Napoleon Pie (page 112) or as a layer of filling between the cake and vanilla filling layers of Birthday Cake Surprise "Pie" (page 107).

Makes 2 cups

1   cup fresh blackberries, raspberries, or strawberries, mashed
1   cup sugar
3   tablespoons cornstarch
½   cup water

In a medium saucepan over high heat, combine the fruit of your choice, sugar, cornstarch, and water. Stir as the ingredients heat to a rapid boil. Boil for about 10 minutes, or until the mixture attains a thick consistency. If you prefer a sauce with no seeds, strain the glacé through a small strainer to eliminate them.

Let the glacé cool to room temperature and then place it in an airtight container and refrigerate for at least 6 hours prior to use.

Glacé can be kept refrigerated in an airtight container for up to a week.

Classic Meringue

Try this with Pumpkin Meringue Pie (page 49) and Lemon-Raspberry Twist Pie (page 121).

Makes approximately 4 cups

4 large egg whites, at room temperature

¼ teaspoon cream of tartar

Pinch of salt

½ cup sugar

1 teaspoon pure vanilla extract

Using an electric mixer set on high speed, beat the egg whites until they become foamy. Add the cream of tartar and salt and continue mixing until soft peaks form. Slowly add the sugar, 1 tablespoon at a time. Once all of the sugar has been added, add the vanilla and beat for 30 more seconds. The meringue should be light and fluffy. Test the meringue to see if it will hold by inserting a spatula into the meringue mixture and quickly pulling it out. If the meringue forms little peaks but does not fall, you have achieved the desired consistency.

Whipped Cream

The following classic recipe for whipped cream can be easily converted into myriad variations with the infusion of accent flavors. Try this basic version with Mixed Berry Crumb Pie (page 26), Lemon Chess Pie (page 36), Turtle Pecan Pie (page 99), and Strawberry Shortcake (page 217), or use to garnish any treat!

Makes 4 cups

2   cups heavy cream

¼   cup confectioners' sugar

1   teaspoon pure vanilla extract

In a medium bowl, using an electric mixer on high speed, combine the heavy cream, confectioners' sugar, and vanilla. Mix for 1 to 2 minutes, or until a creamy consistency is achieved. You'll know it's ready when you can form stiff peaks using a spatula.

For best results, whipped cream should be used immediately.

Chocolate Whipped Cream

Try this with Pastry Cutout Cookies with Raspberry-Almond Cream Cheese Filling (page 152).

Prior to preparation, place a metal bowl in the freezer to chill for at least 15 minutes. Once the bowl is chilled, add to it ¼ cup Chocolate Ganache (page 224) and the ingredients for basic whipped cream. Prepare as directed.

Coconut Whipped Cream

Try this with Lime Pie with Coconut Macadamia Crust (page 123).

½ cup heavy cream
1 teaspoon pure vanilla extract
½ cup cream of coconut (preferably Coco López, found in the mixed-drink section of most grocery stores)

Using an electric mixer on high speed, combine the heavy cream, vanilla, and cream of coconut. Mix for about 1 minute, or until a creamy consistency is achieved. You'll know it is ready when you can form stiff peaks using a spatula.

Maple Whipped Cream

Try this with Maple Custard Pie (page 67), Maple Pecan Pie (page 91), and Maple Pecan Cake (page 193).

Prior to preparation, place a metal bowl in the freezer to chill for at least 15 minutes. Once the bowl is chilled, add to it ½ cup Grade B pure Vermont maple syrup (or more to taste) and the ingredients for basic whipped cream. Prepare as directed.

Marshmallow Fluff Cream

Try this with Graham Cracker Cream Fluff Pie (page 65).

Prior to preparation, place a metal bowl in the freezer to chill for no less than 15 minutes. Once the bowl is chilled, add to it ½ cup marshmallow Fluff and the ingredients for basic whipped cream. Prepare as directed.

Buttercream

Try this with Birthday Cake Surprise "Pie" (page 107).

Makes 2 cups

 6 tablespoons (¾ stick) salted butter, softened
2½ cups sifted confectioners' sugar
 3 tablespoons whole milk
 ¾ teaspoon pure vanilla extract

Using an electric mixer on high speed, beat the butter until it becomes fluffy. On low speed, add the confectioners' sugar, milk, and vanilla. Beat the buttercream for at least 2 minutes, or until it achieves a light, fluffy consistency.

perfect pies & more

Royal Icing

Try this with Sugar Cookies (page 164).

Makes 3½ cups

3 egg whites

2 teaspoons fresh lemon juice

4 cups confectioners' sugar, sifted

Food coloring in color(s) of your choice

Using an electric mixer set on medium speed, beat together the egg whites and lemon juice until they are frothy and well combined. Turn the mixer down to low speed and gradually add the sifted confectioners' sugar, beating it in until the icing becomes smooth.

Test the icing's thickness by dipping a whisk into the icing, removing it, and hanging it upside down over the bowl of icing. You will know the icing is done when it falls off of the whisk into the bowl and remains on top of the surface of the icing for a few seconds before disappearing into the bowl of icing. If the drop of icing disappears right away, you know it is too thin and will run off of the cookies once you begin icing.

As soon as the icing is finished, divide it into small bowls and use food coloring to create your favorite colors.

How Do I Adjust the Icing's Consistency?

If the icing is falling off the edge of the cookies, you know it's too thin. To thicken icing, simply add more confectioners' sugar as necessary. You will know the icing has achieved the perfect thickness when you can use a knife to spread the icing right out to the edge of the cookie without any dripping over.

Acknowledgments

A huge thank you to my editor, Pamela Cannon, for always going above and beyond the call of duty and for supporting not only my writing endeavors but also Michele's Pies in general. Thanks to the stellar team at Random House, including Penelope Haynes, Anna Bauer, Diane Hobbing, Mark Maguire, and Alison Masciovecchio. To my agent, Coleen O'Shea, for constantly staying on top of everything, always being there, and making sure everything runs smoothly. To the talented Ben Fink—it was fabulous to work with you once again. Not only are your photographs beautiful but, as always, I learned so much about food styling just from watching you in action. Thanks to David Venable and the *In the Kitchen with David* team at QVC for all of their support. And to Nikki Van Noy, a dear friend both personally and professionally, who has guided me through this project every step of the way.

I am grateful for my staff at Michele's Pies, who make my vision a reality on a daily basis.

Thanks to my good friend, Gina O'Sullivan, who is unfailingly there to help out with everything from photography for the shop to filling in during the Thanksgiving rush to partaking in memorable travel adventures.

I can't thank the Stuart family enough for their enthusiasm, encouragement, and guidance.

Index

About the Author

MICHELE STUART is the owner and pastry chef of Michele's Pies in Norwalk and Westport, Connecticut. Her pies have earned her twenty-seven first place National Pie Championship Awards in a range of categories. Stuart and her pies have been featured in the *New York Times* and on *Good Morning America* and the Food Network, among other media outlets She lives in Connecticut with her husband and two sons.